Path of Trinity

Cover art by Carlo Difresa and photo by John Black Photography. Final images used with permission from The Engaged Zen Foundation Zen Karmics™ Credit to M for editing diligence and to Rowan Tepper for editing insights. Special credit to Neil Schaller for making this project possible.

ACKNOWLEGEMENTS

I want to thank my mother for her faith and unceasing belief in my mission, and my sister for her dedication.

Last but not least, thank you, Jack-a-Roo, you have been my constant companion.

DEDICATION

To the unknown, unacknowledged and forgotten Saints of the world.

Table of Contents

Chapter 1

Origins: Missouri, and a Basic Introduction to the Problem

"Anyone who brings anything but the King James Bible to this church will be escorted to the door," shouted our pastor, his lanky body leaning out over the pulpit, the veins in his neck bulging. His sermon, "Hell of Hells" was a hit on the Ozarks revival circuit, as was his slide show, "Satanism and Rock Music." It was 1994 in the hills of Southern Missouri.

I have fond memories of hoedowns and fishing excursions on a little creek in the shadow of Assumption Abbey, a Trappist monastery. We Holiness folk didn't know what to make of them. We just thought they were strange. They were strangers, after all, and they kept to themselves. Down there in the hills, different means strange, and all outsiders were strange. As kids, we got up to all kinds of trouble, but the monks never came out, not even just to see the spectacle or hear the laughter. Trappists are not evangelicals, to put it mildly. Only twenty years later would I read Thomas Merton's writings for the first time and realize the richness of this contemplative tradition hidden just on our doorsteps, in the hills of the Ozarks.

My mother would eventually be forced by my father to accept the pastor's fiery sermons and go to his house to apologize for voicing her view that other versions of the Bible were just as inspired. There would also be domestic violence in the home as my father brought to bear the pastor's teaching on breaking the spirit of unsubmissive wives. And I would return from Christian missionary work as a teacher in Moscow to try to moderate the crisis in their marriage. I would not succeed. Neither would I return to missionary work ever again. These experiences would cause me to leave Christianity, eventually becoming an alcoholic.

But before turning to harmful substances— and even becoming briefly homeless— I would get an honors degree in religion and go to graduate school to study religious and cultural theory. I would take a crack at breaking the codes that produced cultural pathologies and made religions such as ours toxic; however, by then I would let my addictions take hold of me and would burn out, leaving UvA Amsterdam without my PhD.

It is common knowledge that you have to hit rock bottom to rise again. My rock bottom happened in Nice, France, on the French Riviera. I had been the Academic Manager in a prestigious language school for the rich in the Carre d'Or of Nice, had a beautiful office in a villa one block from the famed Promenade des Anglais. My dog, Jack, greeted students and had the run of the place. Life was good. I was teaching, doing what I loved.

However, no sooner was I comfortable then I was again out of a job, working the night shift in a hotel in a dodgy part of the city, throwing out the odd drunk in the early morning hours. One evening I myself came home drunk and, while stumbling up the marble stairs to my apartment, slipped and landed squarely on the pointed tip of the spiral staircase, throwing me into a seizure. I woke up in the Nice hospital, severely concussed. I was a bloody mess, and when I got out, I eventually lost even my low-skilled, night-shift job because I was no longer able to navigate the reservation software. It finally got so severe that I ended up a temporary resident in the Antibes mental hospital, on French disability.

This was rock bottom.

Over the preceding decades, I had visited over thirty countries and lived in many them. I had worked in international trade and had been a detective in London, a crime analyst in Washington DC, had crewed yachts in Monaco. I had lived in the world's capitals and in places many people dream of visiting; Beverly Hills, Pebble Beach, Paris. However, these journeys were sadly only an externalization of an inner sense of homelessness that came from being torn from the roots of my faith, *déraciner* from the Christianity of my youth. I was in a state of spiritual fugue, lost.

I spent all of these years profoundly unhappy, sick at my core.

This book is a product of the internal dislocation and illness I have witnessed and experienced, and for which I have found healing. My experiences, my story, transcend the particularity of my own life-history. They bear witness to the pathologies of the present time, which are manifest in manifold ways. It is an attempt to diagnose a spiritual ailment of our world and to propose a solution in theological-practical terms, with dedicated practice applications.

Put simply: what I have to tell you in the following book is a true story. No fabrications. Just the naked truth. I will tell you how not to become a failed saint.

I will share what it is like to climb up the ladder of Divine ascent only to be knocked off and land on your head. I will share meditation and prayer disciplines that can sustain your spiritual life and will offer a theology that heals the psychological splits that have produced unhealthy forms of Christianity. It's not a story with a Hollywood ending, or anything you will hear from a self-help guru, but there is something to be learned.

In our contemporary world, Christianity has in many ways gone astray, and no longer truthfully represents the life and teachings of Christ. Organized religion is in decline, as is church membership and attendance. Religion has taken on the appearance of empty ritual, mainly because the spiritual life of the church does not equal the spiritual need. Naturally, people are compelled to look elsewhere for their spiritual sustenance. The salt has lost its savor, but we cannot live without the life of the Spirit.

In the age of the 'prosperity gospel,' and church-as-entertainment-venue, there is no longer a contemplative life, no evident depth in the faith of Protestant America. Naturally, this turns away people who observe various forms of Christian churches from outside. As the culture wars continue, Evangelical Protestantism as it is practiced in contemporary America is becoming barely recognizable as a branch of the church. It is a branch that is seriously ill, and doesn't even realize it.

When the church fails to exercise the Love of Christ, it views other religions with intolerance and disdain. When it fails to be a Light of the World and put into actual practice the Sermon on the Mount, it rejects the social policies of secular liberalism and socialism.

An analogous term for this in psychology and psychoanalysis is "projection," because as the church is sick instead of dealing with its problems as an institution and as a body of believers, it places this negativity onto those on the outside, and in the worst cases can result in scapegoating. Our country is following a path of deepening spiritual toxicity, as the church fails to undergo a fundamental renewal and fails to see the problem for what it is, where it is. A crisis is coming.

As an antidote to this spiritual pathology, this book puts forward practical, applied theology in a way that can help people as individuals to develop, integrate, and then deepen an inner spiritual life that will heal the psychic split that causes the problem of projection within the individual, and thus within the church.

It is time for the church to enter into an era of spiritual disciplines, into an age of inner health based on prayer and meditation that can be the foundation for 21st Century reformation and revival. But before we look at this, we must go back to the origins of Christianity to find the inner truths of the tradition again and to untangle it from the gnarled threads of the over 2,000 different denominations and faith traditions that represent it today.

Chapter 2

Early Christianity and the Bible

Few Christians know that there were also many Christianities in the first and second centuries after Christ's death. There were many conflicting accounts, and Gospels alleged to be from many of Christ's disciples, from Judas to Mary Magdalene, which did not make it into the New Testament, whereas others did. Some of the many epistles allegedly written by Saint Paul made it into the New Testament, and some did not, such as III Corinthians. Although Saint Paul's writings make up much of the New Testament, many in his own time disagreed with him, just as his texts were arguably inconsistent with each other.

Similarly, there were Christians who were passionate missionaries who did not believe that Jesus was born Divine, and others thought that he became Divine, while still others believed that he was Divine but not human, or that the God of the Old Testament was therefore not the true God. Still others thought that Jesus was a great prophet. Some were even unconcerned with the question of whether or not he was resurrected and did not find this central to their faith.

In fact, it took over 300 years —to put this in perspective, it took about 100 years longer than the United States has been a country— and much arguing before a Roman emperor finally called a council to get the leading contenders to choose a doctrine. It would be nearly 400 years before the Catholic Canon (the accepted books of the Bible) would be agreed upon, which most Protestant churches use. However, this is only one among numerous other Christian canons still used by faithful Christians today. Those who lost the textual arguments in the first four centuries are sadly lost to history.

Some of these were early church fathers and saints who lost their lives for the Christian faith, burnt at the stake or eaten by lions along with their brethren whose ideas eventually became the foundation for the doctrine of the church and for the beliefs of most of the church today. Even many of those whose very teachings formed the core theology of the church today were likewise abandoned by future generations.

It is for this reason that it is essential for us to be prepared to separate ourselves from what we have heard from Christians in our own age and to look to the ancient past for answers. To arrive at truth, we are obliged to revisit the views of the early Christians. In this book, I will be putting forward theological solutions that are consistent with the thinking of the 1st century, which is also compatible with the words of Christ. Indeed, to tap the core of Christian faith and revitalize the tradition, we must first dig to its foundations to find the truth. Shall we do this together? Many scholars assure us that we can.

These scholars tell us that except for the Gospel of Matthew, all of the gospel stories of the New Testament include specific texts that are the same. Most of these were written down not by the disciples themselves but by persons who lived within a hundred years after Christ's death, and who wrote with the pseudonym of a disciple to put down what they had heard from the oral traditions that came from different disciples. This was a common practice in ancient times. Scholars have compiled these sayings into a document called "Q Source." One of the Gospels not included in the New Testament, The Gospel of Thomas, also came from this source and is as old or older than some of those in the New Testament. This is just one example of the rich texts that are lost to our practice today.

Many wise, inspired Christians lived after Christ, and their words too, the wisdom of the faithful and of the Saints, will ground us in our journey into Christian mystical practice. Tradition is important, but it is most important to live the vital truths that are hidden underneath the outer garment of tradition, to fully awaken and climb the ladder of Divine ascent.

- *Bart D. Ehrman. Lost Christianities: The Battles for Scripture and the Faiths We Never Knew. Oxford: Oxford University Press, 2005.*

Chapter 3

Early Christian Mysticism

As I suggested at the outset, one of the things that drives this book, both in theology and practice applications, is the question: "how do we best live out our Christianity and deepen our spiritual life, in the context of the culture wars that have damaged the real heart and the value of religious and spiritual practice?" A few glimpses of insights into the answer have begun to take shape. To facilitate their growth into understanding and practice, we will now need to explore the question, "what is Christian mysticism?"

Put very simply: mysticism is the belief in, and practice of, experiencing God directly, and in some cases of reaching union with God. Over the last 2,000 years, many different schools and approaches have emerged, but one of the common features in the inner practices of Christianity is the belief that you can become divine, which in the Christian tradition usually means to become one with God. In the Eastern Orthodox Christian tradition this is called "theosis," and in the Christian Gnostic tradition this is related to the idea of "gnosis," that is, the direct knowledge of God.

The Christian Gnostics were a large and widespread group of Christians in the early centuries that practiced mystic disciplines. One of the early Christian legends is that the disciple Thomas, with whom is associated the Gospel of Thomas, went as a missionary to India. There are indeed, strong parallels between Christian Gnosticism and Eastern mystical practices.

However, few people are aware of the pervasive influence that Jewish mysticism had on early Christianity. Christian mysticism did not have its primary origins in Greek thought but instead came directly from its Jewish roots. Many of the Jewish mystical texts were written by early Christians (EO p. 53), and the experiences of the sainted elder in Christianity directly correlates and follows from the tradition of the transfigured person who experiences God in Judaism (EO p 62).

In fact, in many cases, it is virtually impossible to distinguish mystical texts from the first centuries as being either Christian or Jewish (EO p. 80). The Jewish mystical literature from that time insists that God can be both seen and unseen (EO p. 116), experienceable and unknowable. Many centuries later, interpretations of this simple logical paradox would become one of the things that separated the Catholic church from the Orthodox, dividing the two largest Christian traditions.

The Jewish tradition of experiencing God passes into Christian thought through the early church father Justin Martyr and from him to Origen, finally becoming the Greek Orthodox doctrine of essences and energies, which is the basis for Christian mysticism in the East (EO p. 121). The essence of God is the unknowable and the uncreated, whereas the energies are the knowable and created through which we can know God *noetically*, that is, intuitively and directly.

As St John Damascene states, "all that we say positively of God manifests not his nature but the things about his nature." Although I have merely scratched the surface of this rich doctrine here, for our purposes we need only to know that the Jewish mysticism of Christ's time forms a basis for Christian mysticism today.

Following the collapse in France...

Shortly after leaving France due to ill health I went to live at the Green Gulch Zen Farm community in California for five months in order to recover my health. As a result of the intensive meditation and supportive community I became well, even better than well; the periods of mediation had radically changed me. I was still in a state of heightened consciousness when an old friend in Houston had a stroke, and so I went to assist him as he recovered. During this time I had been visiting a Carmelite convent for mass and had also attended the Houston Quaker community, seeking spiritual sustenance and guidance. Through these experiences, I was beginning my return to my lost faith.

One day while sitting on a park bench I was overcome with a feeling of joy and sadness and felt the presence of complete and purified love and kindness. At this moment, a poem by Verlaine called "Colloque Sentimental" popped into my mind. It's about two old lovers that meet on a park bench, now in eternity, and the one asks the other "do you remember the ecstasy of our love, does your heart still beat for me?" And I remembered. I remembered the relationship with Christ that had taken me as a young man into the jungle as a missionary, remembered the days of my crisis of faith over seeing my family fall apart. I started crying.

The next day I document the following...

I was having one of my illness episodes and was bed-bound during the day. At some point that day I was lying on the floor and fell into a kind of swoon. I was immobile, it was like I was glued to the floor, and then I felt as though two angels were lifting me. Together, we went through a great deal of dark space and we came to a golden sphere that was shimmering. I went to go through the radiating waves of light, but there were kinds of hard and shard-like golden energy blasts. Then the angels left me to go through on my own. When I came through I was on a golden sphere where there were geometrical dwelling spaces, and I suddenly appeared behind an Ancient on a throne and was to his right, and on his right there was a suspended, purple ruby, and a cherub in static animation. The Ancient had a long white beard and I felt a calm intensity, then the intense feeling that I could not stay there any longer, like I could not hold on to being in that intensely purified space, and so I moved to another side of the golden sphere and I saw more geometric dwellings but no other beings besides the one cherub. I could not or was not able to hold on any longer and came back into my body.

One thing that bothered me as I tried to understand the experience that day, was that there was nothing growing there, there were no flowers, there was no natural life. And so, I began meditating in an attempt to explore this observation. Deep in meditation, I saw a flat, golden place, and then, I perceived a crack from which emerged a tiny flower in a fractional amount of dirt. Strangely, it did not feel exactly right that this should happen. It felt like something was broken, indeed like something had cracked. Perhaps the feeling was that it would hurt to have or take that flower, and even that there was pain in its original emergence. This revealed to me something about the problem of life, which is that imperfection is necessary for life to exist. Where I had been in the vision w⸙

static and golden, fixed and unchangeable. So fixed that I felt a kind of discomfort. It bothered me to feel that there was no imperfection, no movement, or at least what I feel like is life. It felt like I could not be there very long.

It has been a couple of years since I documented this vision, and as I now read over material that was unknown to me then, I have found a correlation to this experience. There is a unique emphasis within the Merkavah mysticism of the 1st century, on what is called "throne mysticism," or, the idea of 'going to the throne' in a vision. I did not realize this then, but it makes sense now, especially since at the time I had wondered why I saw only the back of God in the vision. In the Merkavah tradition, the back of God is associated with God's Glory rather than with Judgment, and in the Christian tradition of the time, which was fused with Judaism, it was also associated with Christ, which is seen as God's Mercy (EO p. 116, p. 301).

In further reflection about this vision journey, I have also learned something about the problem of evil and the difficulty of Creation. Creation is moving from the stasis of perfection and pure consciousness to process and change, difference and differentiation, less and more, and change itself is painful. Creation is an ultimate, entirely participative iteration of the word "Yes." I'm sure somewhere along the line there has been regret at every level of consciousness, but a final and constant "Yes" is necessary, for both God and for humankind.

We must ￼ refore, join with and accept the effects of becoming entirely one wi￼ of the Divine in creating humans and the world. When we create ￼e Divine suffering, that is, we crucify Divinity. When we ￼e gifting, of saying "Yes," then the natural effect of this is self-emptying and gifting into the universe, the ultimate effects of giving life. What we see on the cross can also be seen in the pathos of Mary, his mother, in the originary pain of all creation. To truly live, therefore, is to live the beauty of imperfection, to participate in the very change that gives birth to worlds, to have mercy.

- *Rachel Kevern. From Enoch to Origen: the Jewish Mystical Origins of the Eastern Christian Doctrine of the Mystical Vision of God. Birmingham: University of Birmingham 2007*

Chapter 4

Christian Mysticism in the Inner Tradition

There are many forms of mysticism that have existed in the history of Christianity, but in this book we are following a line that flows through the heart of Christianity and falls mostly within the traditions of Christian Kabbalism and Christian Hermeticism, also known as Inner Christianity, or the Christian Esoteric Tradition. At the end, I will share related practice applications from Jewish Mysticism and Christian Orthodoxy, both of which date back to ancient times.

To begin this discussion of the inner tradition, we will consider the transmigration of souls and a journey to hell. Bear with me. There are many insights to be derived from a careful examination of the way these concepts have manifested in the thought of early mysticism. Most Christians will be surprised to learn that among the early church fathers are those who believed in the transmigration of souls, i.e., the ascent of the soul to God over lifetimes. What inner Christianity teaches is that salvation does not necessarily find its fulfillment in one lifetime, but I will later argue, that it must and can.

This hidden tradition follows from the early church father Clement of Alexandria through his student Origen, and then to us today and is central to understanding esoteric Christianity in the West. Saint Augustine suggests it, but then resists thinking about it, saying "Who, I say, can listen to such things? Who can accept or suffer them to be spoken?" (The City of God, Book XII, Chapter XX). This is because the teaching puts an enormous burden of responsibility upon the Christian to seek inner purification, and involves the fear that this might be an indeterminate process. Saint Jerome, however, mentions it being part of an inner teaching of the church, "The transmigrations of souls was taught for a long time among the early Christians as an esoteric and *traditional doctrine* which was to be *divulged to only a small number of the elect*." (Saint Jerome, Letter to Demetrias).

Saint Gregory (257-337 AD) is perhaps most clear, "It is absolutely necessary that the soul should be healed and purified, and if it does not take place during its life on Earth, it must be accomplished in future lives." (Trinick 1950: 38). Gregory of Nyssa (c.331-c. 396), one of the four great fathers of the Eastern Church, gives us the most clarity on the matter by putting it in the context of salvation: "The resurrection is no other thing than 'the re-constitution of our nature in its original form'," and observes that there will come a time, "when the complete whole of our race shall have been perfected from the first man to the last." (On the Soul and Resurrection).

This belief in the eventual purification and reunification of man also finds a correlation to Jewish mysticism in the belief in a return to perfected man before the fall of creation. In the Jewish mystical tradition the concept of *gilgul*, the transmigration of souls, is part and parcel of the doctrine of the "Tikkun Olam," the repair and redemption of the created world. Christ himself stated that John the Baptist was Elijah come back, and when Christ was asked who he himself was he responded with a question rather than suppressing the belief (Matthew 16:15). Jewish rabbis of his day taught the transmigration of souls, as they still do to this day. However, this implicit understanding has disappeared from Christianity because Christ's message makes the literal truth of this potentially inconsequential.

Few people realize, truly, the point at which their soul passes through this life in a position of high jeopardy. This is why salvation is imperative. There is everything to lose, not just your life, which is temporal, but also your soul.

The belief in heaven and hell has not disappeared entirely from the Christian tradition, some version of which we find in all the faiths of the West. It is important to realize that within the two thousand years of Christian tradition, there are many accounts of those who have seen or otherwise experienced or intuited "hell," or if you will, a hellish state; there are those who have prayed souls out of such hell, Saints and surely more who are no doubt unknown and nameless persons, now lost to history. In what follows I will share a vision that illustrates one way this can happen.

Some months later I had the following vision ...

Over a year after my awakening at Green Gulch Zen Farm I was told in a dream that I would suffer, that I would die, in the coming days. I did not understand this, but I felt sick for five days in a deep spiritual suffering, confined to my room, vacillating between deep spiritual agony and also elation.

On the last day, I went into a vision state and perceived that I was being taken to a wide portal of some sort held open by two angels; I descended into it, descended downwards, and found someone that I had seen in dreams, even years before, as a suffering child on a playground. I brought her up out of there with me, and she became herself again, a woman. I realized that she was someone I had known and loved in another life.

Then I perceived that I was going down again to get someone I had also seen in dreams, a kind of Christian knight, perhaps like an inquisitor, who I somehow knew had tortured a man some 800 years ago. As I drew near to him I saw that he was in a state of suffering, searching in a medieval church library for books that would give him the answers, then trying to escape in the enclosed darkness of the external courtyard. I was frightened to bring him out, worrying that he would again cause destruction, but I took the risk, and as I ascended, he turned to ash and into peace, transforming into a marble coffin. When I surfaced, the angels asked me if I felt these hellish cycles of suffering should exist, and I said, No!

There are a few things that I can draw from this besides the fact that I deeply loved someone, a child or a lover from my past. One thing I am prompted to consider is the notion of *retrocausality*. The past can be addressed, dealt with, perhaps we can shift history, but not without creating a rupture of sorts in eternity. The eternal return of the soul, the lifting from hell, the sometimes falling from heaven, this is all part of the process of the transmigration of the soul, the heightening, or resurfacing of a soul over lifetimes.

In many spiritual traditions there are also some who come back from heaven to fulfill a mission in this world; in Buddhism they are called Bodhisattva, and in the Jewish mystical tradition this is related to the *ibur* of the *tsadik,* that is, the incarnation of a righteous person who has already lived a life on earth but chooses to join another soul on its journey. These are usually difficult tasks and may require a life of suffering. Elijah, who Christ said was John the Baptist come back, similarly experienced suffering as a result of his calling (Mt. 16:15).

In the Christian tradition, we are called to be an embodiment of Christ. Some have been said to be so joined with Christ that they physically presented with the stigmata, the wounds of Christ. When Saint Paul says, "it is not I who live but Christ in me" (Galatians 2:20), this is arguably what he is talking about, and this is what it is to be a Christian Saint; it's what we are supposed to be. But, as we shall see later, we have to be completely on the Path of the Son for Christ to live in us in this way. Presently, we have established that we must bear our trials with patience and *long-suffering*. We may never know what good it has done.

In short, we are doing this together, and heaven and hell taken together are like two turning wheels encircling each other, releasing and refining souls unto eternity. I firmly believe that these *container worlds*, the hells, these states of disorienting descent, will eventually be destroyed; but hell in this current life, is finally that of our own making. The impurities that we do not purify through effort and grace, those from which we are not redeemed, finally condemn us into the essential states of our worst experiences, into the hell-loops of our own negativity and basest desires, sometimes into actual variations on or repetitions of the worst sequences in our life, in which we are spun away from our core, away from the very heaven we might otherwise deserve.

The philosopher Friedrich Nietzsche caught a glimpse of the transmigration of the soul in this sense. What he saw was a soul stuck in lifetimes of unlearning where the return of the soul involves repetitions of failing similar tests or, alternatively, that of one falling into the hell-realms where repetition can sometimes be unchangeable. He was therefore very nearly correct in this simple illustration, "What, if some day or night a demon were to steal after you into your loneliest loneliness and say to you: 'This life as you now live it and have lived it, you will have to live once more and innumerable times more' [...] Would you not throw yourself down and gnash your teeth and curse the demon who spoke thus?" (The Gay Science, §341).

Nietzsche understood something here, and had part of a right response, which is to say an unequivocal "Yes" to life. You must not fall into the negative or you will continue to descend; however, in order to enter into redemption, you must experience a fundamental turning. In the Greek, this is called *metanoia*, meaning, a transformative change of heart. Metanoia is commonly translated as "repentance" in the English language, which is related to redemption in the Christian tradition. We will discuss this in a later chapter.

What Nietzsche's demon was describing was a negative loop of repetition, precisely what I had seen in hell. The natural recoil we have from entertaining this truth is the very reason Saint Augustine reacted to these inner teachings, "Who can accept or suffer them to be spoken?" (City of God, Book 12: Ch. XX). Of course, just because we may find this most difficult of truths hard to bear does not mean that it should not be spoken. People must be woken from their spiritual slumber, and to do otherwise is to risk their souls.

The notion of the reality of the other worlds involves that which is infinitely more complex, more beautiful, and more horrible than our own. We have every reason to fear the kind of hell I've described, but this fear will not keep us from it. In anticipation of what I will develop below, it is not fear, but it is only dwelling in love, entering into constant acts of self-purifying, and into the surrendered redemption of divine grace, that we *ascend.*

This life is an ascent of the DNA of our soul. As mysterious as that sounds, it is merely the recognition of the true spiritual uniqueness and purpose within each soul, that seeks to be revealed as we make every decision. But even those who have risen can fall again, and it is through imperfection that we learn some of the greatest lessons, which is something I hope will become clear as I continue to share my own story.

- *Richard Smoley. Inner Christianity: A Guide to the Esoteric Tradition. Shambala Publications, 2002.*
- *Valentin Tomberg. Meditations on the Tarot: A Journey into Christian Hermeticism. Tarcher Perigree: 2002.*

PART II. Crisis and Transformation

Tangible Reflections: An introduction

In Part I, we looked briefly at spiritual problems in the church today and anticipated that the church will need a new kind of revival that is focused on the intensive spiritual disciplines of meditation and prayer. We looked at the early church, and learned about the richness of Christianity's inner tradition, drawing promising insights into well-being and growth. We also looked at the connections between Jewish and Christian mysticism in the first century, including their shared views on the transmigration of the soul. I shared my personal experiences of a kind of ascent into heaven and descent into hell that correlates with these ancient traditions. We finally looked at how imperfection is a necessary result of Creation and is our shared responsibility.

In Part II, we will look at the lived experience of *being-in-relationship* and how this is essential to spiritual health. We will compare Christianity's view of the self-as-real to Buddhism's view of the empty self, and compare and contrast the two traditions. We will then look at the process of awakening, illuminating ways in which spiritual disciplines can produce this, and I will give some tips on how to navigate this complex but crucial terrain. Finally, we will bring this section to a close by looking at redemption in the Christian tradition.

Chapter 5

Ascent

Some months before the visions and while still living on the Zen monastery...

I'm sweating profusely as I put one foot in front of the other with determined precision, the eroded gravel and red dirt slipping under my feet as I climb the steep ascent, the sea below me. At my back is Muir Beach and the valley, a solitary pub and some grazing horses. The sky is overcast and over the hill is the sea again, and the San Francisco Bay. As I gather myself to keep climbing, suddenly a voice in my mind says, "turn around, look behind you!" I do, and at my back is a beautiful rainbow, arching over the entire valley.

In a flash, leaping up out of my flushed exhaustion, was something amazing: an entire heightening of my being, as big as the valley, as big as the rainbow. This was it! This was the "salvation experience" I had longed for. This was what I had sat months in meditation on the monastery hoping for! All the colliding experiences and struggles of a lifetime resolved in a moment of complete density of being, collapsed in the single-pointed awareness of my body, this valley, and the arch of a rainbow.

When I had arrived at the Zen community months before, I was a broken person. It took every ounce of my energy to get up at 4:00 am to mediate, and endure meditation intensives sometimes lasting six hours or more a day. It took everything I had just to perform my work-related tasks in the community. And even then, I have fond memories of being with friends and chanting sutras throughout the night to herald in the new year, the odors of incense rising in the dim light of the zendo as we sat together, finally getting up and doing our last sampai of the day.

Not long after the periods of deep meditation and the 'rainbow awakening,' I started having more amazing experiences. I fell into the 'synchronicity of being.' That is, I started anticipating what would happen next. In my head I would suddenly think of someone, could count "one, two, three" and then there was so-and-so, rounding the corner. One person in the kitchen once asked me, "are you reading my mind?" Not really, it wasn't quite like that, even though somehow, I knew what this person wanted, where her thoughts had turned.

Once I thought to myself, "that person looks sad, I need to smile and bow when she comes up to me," and even though I had never had her do exactly this before, she beat me to the punch, smiling and bowing ahead of my intended action!

In this synchronous state, one is continually turning through, and being turned by, the reality around them. That is to say, if you are in a synchronous state, you are entering into an experience of *interbeing*. It sounds deep, but in truth, nothing has changed; in fact, this is the way it always is, it's just that you have become aware of this reality in real time, and can *move* with it!

Like walking a tightrope, when you begin to think about it, you can fall into the problem of over-thinking or delusion, or both. It is only by looking straight forward and staying in the immediate moment that you remain in clear transcendence. Your mind has to play catch-and-release all while living in this intensity, and it has to do so without attachment. It is precisely as described and cautioned about in the Jewel Mirror Samadhi, "turning away and touching are both wrong, it is like a mass of fire." This text is a brilliant, poetic rendering of the process of awakening. Awakening is indeed neither "turning away," nor "touching," because if you walk away from the experience you lose it, but if you cling to it you lose it as well.

A story is also told in a *Genjokoan*, about a Zen master with a fan, who sits and just fans himself, but who in this simple gesture communicates ultimate truth to his students. In the awakening state that might result from this, you might begin to experience yourself as a prime-mover in the flow of interdependence as it is coming to you, and you can shift with it. But being in this altered state is as easy as it is complicated! To extend the above metaphor, upon awakening it starts out with, "what's all this fanning going on" and then "who is fanning who" and "am I ahead or behind the fanning?" The "I'm just fanning" happens again, later, once a new center of being has been realized.

While sitting in samadhi, trauma would often surface. Then, it would be cathartic bursts of humor that rose to the top; it was like quantum psychotherapy at high speed, mental obstacles of a lifetime were manifesting, sometimes dissipating, in just one setting. Of course, at some point, this can get all tangled up, and thus, one must learn grounding-techniques and concentration methods. These can be learned supportively by someone who has been though the awakening process, which is almost invariably messy. The

Scottish psychiatrist R.D. Laing once rightly observed, "the mystic and the schizophrenic swim in the same oceans, but whereas the one swims, the other drowns." This is a real risk, and something we will look at later.

Not surprisingly, then, as you continue in this experience, you enter into what the Genjokoan calls "delusion beyond delusion," that is to say, once you are in an awakened state in order to resolve deep spiritual issues and barriers to living complete truth, your mind runs scenarios regarding the reality around you which often produce incorrect but useful internal narratives. You, therefore, have to hold this in "suspension in disbelief" and allow them to play out internally in catharsis and resolution, or even into revelations, in order to arrive at inner health.

In short, you have to pass through delusions that go beyond the normal waking ones in which we function, more or less well, in order to go through a reset process. Although I will treat this in greater depth in Part III, it is worth saying here that if you choose to pursue this, and are not adequately supported during this phase, you will potentially collapse or be overwhelmed; always be sure to practice in a skilled and supportive community.

After these experiences, and following reaching a level of inner clarity, I started having 'precognitive dreams.' I would dream the events of the next day or coming days in layered metaphors, and then see them actually happen. These anticipations were difficult to navigate, as some of them would happen regardless of my thoughts, whereas it seemed that over others I held the power of change and decision. These are the true decision points the Jewish mystic speaks of, the moments of freedom in an otherwise determined reality, or what the Buddhist might say is a *karmic matrix*, which allows a decision-space where you can "catch" the moment and ride it out to a best outcome.

Once I called my sister based on a dream and told her, "sister, you're going to have a difficult and traumatic move soon." Of course she did not know what to think as she was in a stable lease and got on well with the landlord, and so replied that everything was good, there were no problems. Around two weeks later she had exactly the difficult move that I foresaw, but as it turns out what was going to happen happened regardless. Nothing was shifted by my foreknowledge. But in other cases, it seemed that it was. An example of this happened after I left the monastery and went back into the world, but now as a changed person. Some months had passed, and I had worked a long day and was living in a small town in southern Illinois, temporarily lodging in an old railroad house used many years ago by itinerate rail-workers. One afternoon I had the prompting, "go over to the graveyard down the road." And as I follow promptings —but always with discernment— I did just that, taking my little dog, Jack, along. When I arrived I was told, "go to the back of the graveyard." I did that. "Go over to that stone and remember the name." And so I went to the stone and stood there.

Suddenly I felt a great feeling of love, got the message, "get health insurance," then felt free to leave, having noted in my mind the person's name. I did not have any idea who this person was, and so I asked around. It turned out that this person had the same last name as a co-worker and so I asked him if he knew who this was, and he told me, yes, it was his grandfather, and they had been very close. I told him what I had experienced and that he should "get health insurance." He replied, "I'm working on it." As far as I know he followed through and got insurance but then, just a few months later, unexpectedly went into the hospital for what would have been a costly extended stay.

This is just one example of the many experiences that followed. These are some of the results of awakening and staying in heightened conscious, of becoming connected with this complex multiverse that is happening all around us. This can happen spontaneously, as with me on the hill above Muir Valley, but it rarely happens without dedicated, focused, sustained discipline, even though some rare people may be born this way. This is why meditation and prayer is necessary as the prelude to beginning a spiritual ascent.

- *Shōhaku Okumura. Realizing Genjokoan: The Key to Dogen's Shobogenzo. Wisdom Publications, 2010.*
- *John Daido Loori. The True Dharma Eye: Zen Master Dogen's Three Hundred Koans. Shambala Publications: 2009.*

Chapter 6

Christianity versus (or together with) Zen Buddhism: Am I real?

Towards concluding the pamphlet, I will explain some techniques of Zen meditation and recommend it as a practice for awakening. However, one of the challenges in bridging traditions such as Zen Buddhism and Christianity is that you risk ending up on a neutral no-man's-land that does not honor either tradition on its own terms. In the case of Christianity and Buddhism, you risk falling into a non-dualism that invariably favors Zen and is ultimately non-theistic and thus dismisses the truths of Christianity at the ontological level. I will attempt to avoid this.

One relatively mainstream and widespread Western tradition in which the concept of God is most original, influential, and fecund is found in the Jewish Rabbinic and mystical traditions, which one sees at the roots of Christianity. Jewish Rabbinic readings of the Biblical texts, such as the commentaries and exegeses comprising the Midrash, the Aggadah, Halakhah, the Talmud, and Zohar, have always been multi-layered, finding multiple Creation narratives in Genesis, and using the stories to self-transcend the story, that is to go beyond the immediate meanings to much deeper, more significant truths and to produce personal transformation.

In Christianity, the Eastern (or Oriental) Orthodox tradition is exceptional: by contrast to the rational theology of the Roman Catholic Church, it holds the view that God is in everything. Even though this is almost impossible to understand in the analytical mind, a direct experience is achievable through means of contemplative practice because the indwelling Spirit gives life to and lives in all things, even those profane, and all things participate in the life of the Spirit. This is called *panentheism*, as opposed to *pantheism*.

While pantheism claims that God is in everything, panentheism affirms this and adds: all things *are* in God. That is, without God, they would have no being. And this is what the Jewish mystics have believed from Christ's time. Kabbalah, the Jewish mystical tradition, holds that Creation itself was God restricting Himself in his infinity in order to create individual sparks of his being that could exercise free choice and be redeemed finally unto Himself, each of whose essences participated in the very life of all Creation.

What is important to understand here, is that the most ancient elements of the Christian faith traditions correspond to, and are rooted in, the same beliefs as the Jewish mystical understandings of God. And these are also very similar to Buddhist ontology. And yet, the similarity gives way to a difference in emphasis where we observe that Buddhism asserts an even stronger sense in which all things are dependently arising phenomena. There is no independently existing reality, no *noumenon*, or thing in itself. All things are finally empty appearances devoid of selfhood.

Jewish mysticism, and finally perhaps Christian Orthodoxy as well, might similarly agree that in the last account everything is empty and unreal – of anything but God, whose divine essence and energies give birth to and sustain the world in which we exist, but they will still maintain that each of us has, for the indefinite future, a distinct soul.

To make it simple, the difference between the Western traditions and Buddhism is that in Buddhism nothing is real, there is no essential reality, and neither is there anything that could be called a soul. All that we see and experience is actually empty of true being, a co-dependent arising, merely the illusion of essential being. Thus, Buddhism is a non-theistic religion that necessarily holds God to be a mere collective construct and which also denies the reality and identity of the individual soul. According to the doctrines of Buddhism, I am not a real and existing self; rather I am a not-self, an illusory and composite being, a collection of karmic aggregates, component features, with no real core.

Thus for the Zen Buddhist there is neither heaven, nor hell, nor reincarnation, nor the soul. And just as Buddhism lacks a concept of the soul, it also lacks the idea of a divine creator being. Buddhism lacks an ontologically primary, essentially originary basis for this phenomenal ephemeral world, and thus too, any sense of an ultimately affirmative relationship with being, with Divine essence as such.

Unlike Buddhism, Jewish and Christian mysticism maintains that even though suffering is intrinsic to Life, the struggle against suffering is founded upon and aims toward a larger meaning. In this respect, there is a strong kinship and affinity between the Jewish mystical tradition and Orthodox Christian theology.

Buddhism is an effective spiritual science. However, the father of quantum mechanics, Werner Heisenberg, once made a relevant observation, "The first gulp from the natural sciences will turn you into an atheist, but at the bottom of the glass God is waiting for you." Don't stop at awakening. God is waiting for you. Nothing is more intimate to you than God.

"Does it hurt?' asked the Rabbit. 'Sometimes,' said the Skin Horse, for he was always truthful. 'When you are Real you don't mind being hurt.'" The Velveteen Rabbit.

"People have forgotten this truth," the Fox said. "But you mustn't forget it. You become responsible forever for what you've tamed. You're responsible for your rose." The Little Prince

- *Margery Williams. The Velveteen Rabbit, Doubleday, 1991*

- *Antoine de Saint-Exupéry. The Little Prince, Mariner Books, 2000*

Chapter 7

On Being-in-Relationship

When the Jewish philosopher Martin Buber asserted that "all real living is meeting," (I and Thou 1958; 25) he intended something quite profound, something essential about our being-in-the-world. Buber makes an important distinction between treating a person as a mere object, as would a salesperson, i.e., in terms of an instrumental rationality, and considering every person as always-already in relation with us. Such an encounter with the other, is the ground of all possible experience of the Divine.

Consider the doctor-patient relationship. It is useful for the doctor to see the patient as a patient, that is, as someone with health concerns that are specific and need to be treated, or even as a body. However, if both the doctor and the patient only experience the encounter as a matter of dealing with a health issue, experiencing each other primarily in terms of their roles, then something essential is lost, which is the life of the Spirit in each person as well as in the encounter itself. This can be true of something as simple as taking a walk in a forest. I can see a forest as trees or I can experience a forest, a tree, as Divine encounter. Both ways of seeing are necessary to function as a whole person, and both are important.

Sartre and Lacan also make a relevant observation about our way of seeing, which is that our looking at another person, that is turning our consciousness in their direction, can determine their reality. We exist in part in relation to being observed. Another way to see this is that intention carries through in Spirit and affects other souls. Every way of seeing, either positive or negative, disinterested or engaged, is a valuation that impacts. We send energy with each turn of our consciousness. If we can see through to the true self of the other person, which is to say, if we can see them though God's eyes, our gift can be an awesome empowerment. Every look is a prayer.

Only if we exist essentially in relationship with others, can we have a real relationship to God that is as much rooted in the immanence of life as in the transcendence of God. This shift of orientation, that of being-in-relationship, is the basis not only of a healthy spiritual life, but indeed of a mystical encounter with all Being. This understanding can bring much spiritual and psychological well-being, but it is lacking in spiritual practice today, and is symptomatic of our age. Understanding being-in-relationship means acknowledging that the Spirit is in us, and in the in-between; it is the encounter itself through which we become a realized self, a self which treats the other as an instance of God in our lives.

- *Martin Buber. I and Thou. Scribner: 1958.*
- *Kenneth Kramer. Martin Buber's I and Thou: Practicing Living Dialogue. Paulist Press: 2004.*

- *Jean Paul Sartre. Being and Nothingness. Routledge: 1943*

Chapter 8

Tripartite Personhood in Christianity

Whereas Buber taught that the self only becomes real in relationship, Christianity teaches that while this is partially true, we are nonetheless constituted of three parts: a body, a soul, and a Spirit. In this section, I will elaborate on the idea of being-in-relationship as a tripartite person, three distinct parts of the same being. And while the body is temporal the soul is not, and it is from this structure that we function as conscious human beings.

The soul can in some ways be understood as mind, insofar as mind functions as the center of our decision process and focal awareness. Another way to say it is that this is the DNA of our life, which is intimately connected with the souls of others, and capable of many transformations. However, the soul often finds itself in bondage. In Christianity, this can be understood as what is meant by "original sin," and in the traditions of the East, as what is meant by "karma." Being liberated from this bondage is understood in the western traditions as redemption, which not only frees the soul, the true self, but also redeems the soul unto God. The Jewish mystical tradition similarly understands there to be layers of soul that are associated with levels and processes of ascent, which we will look at later.

Another perspective on the soul that will illuminate both its power and its vulnerability is found in natural religions, such as shamanism. In shamanism, there is the concept of "soul loss," which is when your soul becomes shattered, broken up and spiritually disconnected from your lived life. It can descend into the unconscious to put it in psychological terms, or be overtaken by demonic influences, which in the Christian tradition is called "possession." "Possession," in this sense, is importantly different from "oppression," in which the soul maintains its integrity but is assaulted from without. This can also be understood on the psychological level by exploring the disconnect we experience that keeps us from making authentic decisions.

This stifling disconnect can be seen in the effects of living in what the French sociologist Jean Baudrillard called *hyperreality*, the state of mind produced by being overly embedded in technology and in pervasive media that divorces us from our actual lived lives. This produces alienation from the true self and other and can result in a failure of being-in-relationship. We can become alienated from our own essential self, from our soul and Spirit, if we make of ourselves objects and are inauthentic to who we truly are, that is to say we become unreal. This frequently happens though the medium of social media. Similarly, we can also become alienated from our true self by seeing our body as a commodity, as only a tool to get something, for example by sexualizing ourselves in a way that is not what we truly intend toward those around us. A similar lack of mindfulness can compromise our soul and the souls of others and is damaging to our collective psychogeography.

That said, the most common disintegration of the self happens through trauma, grief, overwork, addictions or forms of escapism. All this can produce dissociated states and depression, and in these conditions you often end up functioning only and always determined by all that is around you and operating though you, unable to truly be a conscious agent of your own life. In this state you are fundamentally alienated from your true self and cannot live the Spirit-filled life. You cannot truly live in authentic relationship with others and the world around you. Therefore, being-in-relationship is essential to maintaining healthy integration which can begin to actualize the true self, the soul's essential nature.

The Spirit, on the other hand, is quite literally God in us, is both that which animates our being and also that which guides us into perfected life and liberation, and in this sense we are all one. Spirit is directly participative in the Divine Being as energy and as agency, but as such it is limited by the state of our soul and its choices, by its state of purity and surrender. When we are embodied in Spirit, what naturally flows from this is true being-in-relationship with other people, and when our primary focus in upon being in relationship in this way, we will experience the Spirit in all encounters. Living the life of the Spirit requires that the true self, the soul, be revealed and empowered. We will explore some techniques for this later.

Towards concluding this section, I would like to come back to the idea of the body, in light of what we have learned about the soul. The body can also become divined, which is called transcendence in immanence. This is why some Christians keep the relics of saints. What Saint Paul called "the flesh," on the other hand, is a spiritually detrimental physical activity or related desire, and is connected to the demonic realms. That is to say, some forms of sexual activity can draw you directly down into a hellish spiritual reality. Think of spiritual reality as on a scale of ascent from worldly wisdom to non-rational heavenly truth. Indeed, every higher spiritual truth and practice has a flip negative correspondence, and every wisdom is a flawed interpretation of higher truths. We only see and experience the truth in terms of our spiritual purity. This applies to both spiritual seeing, and to spiritual practice. Sex can actually be a journey of spiritual ascent for two people in a loving and committed covenant with certain disciplines that transcend physical reality whilst also involving it.

Unfortunately, sex has been denigrated in some forms of Christianity. This may in part be a result of Saint Paul's teaching about celibacy, although it often goes unnoticed that he suggests that it is optional to be celibate (1 Corinthians 7:9). However, the idea of celibacy does have merit and can perhaps be best understood as a discussion of sublimation. Because sex is a very powerful human need, second only to food, it is the most difficult spiritual energy to control. The total control and sublimation of this energy, the redirection of this energy, is a supreme source of spiritual power. However, between partners, the ascent is determined by the spiritual level of both people, since their souls are linked. When one is alone and has redirected this energy, there are no restrictions. This, I argue, is a deeper meaning of Paul's teaching.

To summarize, we are three parts, body soul and Spirit, and the objective is to liberate the soul though becoming *in Spirit*, thereby also glorifying both the soul and body. The Spirit-filled life can be realized through being-in-relationship, that is though becoming our true selves by engaging the other as a true case of God in the world as Spirit, both in the other person and in the encounter itself. In this way, we experience God as *in everything*, which leads to deep inner healing and spiritual health. However, as we will see in Part III, living this way and reaching this point requires disciplines of awakening that can be very challenging.

Chapter 9

Descent and Death

I once picked up a book off the shelf in a used bookstore on spirituality called, "After the Ecstasy, the Laundry." What a great title! My title for the following section might be something along those lines but more humbling, "Awakening into way too much Laundry!"

As we saw from the beginning, I had come into awaking from out of years of spiritual torment born of trauma, and this doesn't just disappear when you are awakened. It does for a while, but essentially the spiritual challenge is moved to another level. You might have thought that after an awakening it was all rainbows, that you were suddenly a beautiful person, enlightened and new. I have something challenging to tell you: this is not true. This is instead the beginning of a journey.

In this Chapter, I will be less committed to explicating the philosophical theories at work in this journey, than I will be to articulating my experience in dialogue with you, the reader. In so doing, I hope to begin advocating for your own immersion in the praxis that I myself have encountered.

To begin, we might note that there is a reason that the Buddhist monks take moral vows very early on in their vocation of meditation, and that these are incessantly repeated, which is also true for the monks who live a life of prayer in the West. When you awaken, and here I will use the true metaphor of the chakras, you get them *all lit up!* This includes every part of your being. You need to be prepared for that, because it's going to get messy. Whatever you had to start with may get an initial clean up, but then the challenge just moves up a notch. There can be many outcomes to this, including negative ones.

Because of this complexity, it would not be incorrect to assume enlightened evil exists, which is effectively bending the light to egoic ends from a place of spiritual empowerment and mastery. While this sounds impressive, it is in fact a failure of ascent. King Solomon fell into this trap. Using spiritual laws to shift reality, which you also do inadvertently, becomes a moral complexity of daily life for an awakened person and in some sense this is no different than what people deal with normally. For the awakened person, it's just happening at another level of consciousness and awareness because you have added insight into the immediate and long-term effects of your thoughts and actions.

There is also the problem of judgment, of negativity in discernment, something which has to be brought into check because you will start to see through people all the time which can become irritating; this is to put it mildly in some cases. Saint Paul gave us the best and only solution in saying that you must bring every thought into captivity, into "the Mind of Christ" (2 Corinthians 10:5). You must purify everything immediately with the spirit of compassion, or you will yourself become spiritually toxic and potentially get lost in negativity. And you can also be opened up to spiritual attack.

To illustrate this I will tell you a story.

Some time after leaving the Zen monastery, I was in the prophetic mind of 'cutting discrimination,' something that is sometimes actually required as an inward turning to purification. But in this case I was in this mind as I was having lunch with a friend and his wife and something happened that triggered me; there was a flash of irritation that crossed my mind, and in that very second a glass of water flew off our table and hit the floor, breaking and creating a mess. I immediately realized, again, something I already knew and had been keeping as best I could in check: "what we think in our mind has real effects both in the spirit realm and in the immediate external world."

This is also known as "the laws of attraction," the principle that whatever your hold in consciousness draws to it the same, positive or negative. A deep understanding gives the wise person every reason to hold only kind thoughts! But it's not as simple as it sounds. We don't automatically go from being messed up to cleaned up. There is a natural process of internal cleansing, learning and growing.

Two other things are also important to understand in this context. One is how important it is to be in a spiritual community and following a path, and the second is to understand the significance of soul ties, that is to say, the deep connection we have to others, to spiritual reality and how it determines our awakening, indeed our daily life. This is yet another way to express the crucial significance of Buber's concept of being-in-relationship.

The first thing, and an absolutely essential one, is that your spiritual life is nurtured as part of a community in which you are actively involved. Become part of a dedicated tradition and ensure that your spirituality develops within the broader confines of this dedication. There was considerable spiritual support, both in the physical realm, that is to say in ordinary reality, and in the spiritual realm during my awakening. That is to say, there are saints and ancestors, and even angels, working to help us. When you are part of a community it comes with the support and protection that this involves. And of course, the difficulties too.

When you leave this, either physically or spiritually, when there is alienation, then this source of support and connection is cut off; there is a rupture. This is true of all our relationships, such as one in our place of employment, among neighbors, or in a marriage covenant. Most people can intuitively recognize when they have separated spiritually or emotionally from someone, and some can even know intuitively when there is a death of someone they care about.

When the separation has been traumatic there are often lingering problems that remain. This was true of my separation from Christianity many years ago. I was still angry about it after all those years, even after awakening. I had also left the Buddhist monastery, and so no longer had that connection *or* the positive connection I needed to a Christian community, to one that held my values and understood deep spiritual practice.

What are the results of being in such a spiritual no-man's-land, of believing in God but in the largest possible sense of the word? What comes of this? To approach these questions, and provide context for the following narrative, let us reach way back, and consider a very broad context for the emergence of spiritual practices. Did you know that, just for example, various strains of ancient Egyptian religion date back into prehistory, with a dominant form arising more than 5,000 years ago? That is to say that thousands of years before there was any known monotheism, there was an established spiritual practice.

And before this, hundreds of millions of years before, the earth was populated by trilobites, who were driven into extinction by a catastrophic event, and which were then followed by the age of the dinosaurs, and our own age thus in sequence. All this on our relatively young planet. There are billions of universes out there, within which scientists now assure us there may well be intelligent life similar to our own, including overlapping worlds and parallel realities.

Thinking about this cosmic scope can be overwhelming, and so most people don't ask themselves the question of how this might relate to their faith practice, or if they do, they go into denial almost immediately because they understandably find it difficult to hold in mind the complex implications. God presents Godself in every age. However, we are limited by the determinedness of our essential state, by being human.

This limitation is apparent if we consider this in light of our discussion of the soul. We might think of it in the following way: the Spirit is in all things, throughout universes, but on the individual level we can still do things to grieve the Spirit and withdraw its presence from us as other than life-sustaining, which leads to hell states even in this life. The Spirit guides the soul in its ascent and bears with us our suffering. There is thus nothing more intimate than God who very literally takes this journey with us, yet remains hidden from us, suffering the evil of the world immediately though us. Even in hell there is a fraction of the light of God. On the other side our Spirit contains the imprint of our souls, which is immediately visible, translucent as energy. We are ensouled Spirit. We are, thus, intimately a part of these vast universes and participate in them through the restrictions of our consciousness.

The awakening mind is, therefore, open onto a vast field of knowing and our spiritual being follows according to the laws of attraction, which is particularly dangerous if you are outside a tradition. You have soul ties, deep connections, and may relate to multiple faith traditions, unhealthy sexuality, past trauma, *anything*. It is all there to be dealt with. You get it all handed back to you to process as part of your spiritual learning curve. You will almost certainly enter into a realm of testing and trial. In this, there can be a very real danger, it can become a nightmare lived in waking life.

This is what happened to me.

When I arrived to work a new job in a small hotel in Bloomington Indiana my dreams and visions started to go back into distortion, as they were before their clarification at the monastery. I woke up one night in a night terror, envisioning a succubus on me, almost unable to move. Another night I was tempted as though by some ancient Djinn who tried to penetrate my consciousness, which I resisted. A sexual thorn in the flesh re-emerged with intensity and had to be resisted. I then perceived that someone who had been murdered was also trying to get through to me to tell me what had happened. The barrage persisted for days. Eventually it became so bad, so exhausting, and I was so sleep-deprived that I told myself, "I'm going to drink myself to sleep and finally get a decent night's sleep!" Which I preceded to do, but despite all the alcohol I laid in my bed, lucid, moving between different realms of consciousness, unable to sleep.

At one point that night I went into a vision of a place that looked like Karnak. I had been there, in Egypt, years before. And at this location, I had had a powerful spiritual experience. Now, in my vision, when I looked I saw a griffin near an entryway; he moved away from me, but then a sporty and fit white cat with human legs came up to me— friendly and playful— but at that very moment I felt a great dread, which was the exact word I later noted in my dreambook, and the experience became extremely discomforting. The next day, after a sleepless night, I looked this up. Sekhmet is a cat goddess of ancient Egypt. She is the goddess of drunkenness— how appropriate— and is also known as "the mistress of dread!" Now that was simply crazy! What was I to make of all this, how could I possibly integrate these authentic experiences into one whole? I was getting desperate. Not even drinking worked! In this state I had stopped praying.

But my mother was still praying and was sending me verses about spiritual battle that were exactly what I needed to hear. One night I was having so much distress that I felt that my soul was leaving my body, and in this moment of sheer terror a man in a robe and with a white beard showed up, and I knew, without knowing before who this was: "Padre Pio." I thought I was dying and was anguished, but he told me, "you don't need to smoke" and gave me a blessing. I was then able to sleep. The next day I also looked him up as well and saw that he was a Saint, and that his motto was, "pray, hope and don't worry!" That was just amazing! What did I do when I worried? Smoked.

I have since quit smoking. Saint Pio is my spiritual father and has remained so, this despite my staying an unaffiliated Christian, outside the communion of any specific church. These sacred mysteries, the sacraments, I *respect,* and see them as the outward garments of the inner life. The sign of the cross is extremely powerful, and I use it regularly for protection and to dispel negative influences. This sign is no doubt very ancient and crosses over cultures.

What we can learn from this experience and those preceding them is that it is critical to be grounded in, and protected by, a tradition and by the angelic support that this entails. It has been emphasized how vital it is to be aware of the "laws of attraction" and to purify the mind, to "put on the mind of Christ" in all things. We have seen what can result from not doing that. We have also seen how being open to vast spiritual reality can produce a range of experiences that are not spiritually supportive, but also that spiritual testing, descent, will be part of a process of spiritual heightening, but which involves real dangers.

In the Bible it is commanded, "Thou shalt have no other gods before me" (Exodus 20:2). The obvious inference here is that there are other actual gods, and that it is expedient that our primary relationship not finally be mediated by entities or values, by anything that stands between yourself and direct encounter with God; otherwise you will be determined by these spiritual realities. This is crucial to understand, even as we turn to Saints and others for support, both here and in the Spirit realm (1 John 4:1). To the extent that something, or someone, stands between you and God this will be the limit of your ascent, and the limit of your vision.

However, if you experience distortion in vision, as I shared earlier, this does not necessarily mean that you have fallen spiritually or are under attack. Saint Paul reminds us that we "see but through a glass darkly" (1 Cor 13:12) and flawed revelation is a natural fact of spiritual vision because we will only see with spiritual clarity to the extent that we are purified. Also, there are spiritual laws governing this. Frequently revelation will come in metaphors, in visual puns and humor even, and things will sometimes have the reverse of their meaning, like with the negative of a photo, and therefore can only be discerned by felt inference, and this requires a sense of playfulness. So, just because you see only fractals of the truth should not dishearten you. This does not mean that you are not a spiritual person. And you do not need revelations to ascend.

We will discuss the esoteric Christian meanings of these kinds of experiences, like mine with Saint Pio, and related topics such as being born again, later. We will look at the difference between what in the Protestant Holiness Tradition is called *salvation* and rebirth and purification, or *sanctification*, and death to self. This is something that may need to happen multiple times, as we progress along our spiritual path. As Saint Paul so succinctly put it, "I die daily" (1 Corinthians 15:31). *Entire sanctification*, complete purification, is the eventual result which can finally become *theosis*, deification in the Orthodox Christian tradition.

These initial experiences, however, as we have seen, can potentially result in imperfect outcomes which I will discuss later. What is most important to understand in this chapter is that there is a real danger, and that caution and specific support is necessary.

Unwavering faith in Divine Providence is essential. However, it not necessary to grasp the language I have shared to have powerful experiences that begin a spiritual journey! These can happen to anyone!

- *Stanislov Grof. Spiritual Emergency: When Personal Transformation Becomes a Crisis. Tarcher Perigree: 1989.*

Chapter 10

Redemption

The great question that is common to all Abrahamic religions, a question that forms the core of the Christian faith, is posed with great urgency and simplicity is the question of "*how can or will we be redeemed?*" It is in the answer to this fundamental question of faith that differentiates the Jewish and the Islamic faiths from the Christian one; and once again, between the Roman Catholic, and the Eastern Orthodox Churches.

The Jewish mystic answers this by saying it is in little moments of free choice over lifetimes in which we purify ourselves and earn heaven or, one might add, hell. A member of the Eastern Orthodox Catholic church might say, according to the Christus Victor view of atonement, "it is according to following in Christ's steps and reaching *theosis*." The Evangelical Baptist would say, according to the considerably later view of redemption, i.e., the penal substitution theory, "it's by confessing your sins and accepting Christ into your heart, and thereby you are saved from God's wrath." There are many variations on these, each of which has scriptural support.

However, through experience I maintain something somewhat different. I hold the position that it is by getting close enough to the Love of God, and dwelling in this love continually, moment by moment, that God will help you and extend Grace. This requires not one choice but many.

As we saw in the section above concerning crisis and transformation, it is essential to stay within a tradition, but this does not mean that you must be bound by belief in only one of the many variations on redemption found within the Christian tradition. It is also possible to hold more than one view simultaneously, though non-rational knowing or *gnosis*, that is, through experience. Consequently, my view is that redemption is an ongoing process; it is not a one-time deal, but something that is accessible through love and being-in-relationship. I am grateful for all those who have contributed to my own redemption, who have been the Christ in every person I have met. We are all in this together.

As I will share later, personal transformation, crisis, is part of an ongoing spiritual process that requires an unfailing faith in Divine Providence and also an understanding that you "must take heed lest you fall." (1 Corinthians 10:12) and continue to "work out your salvation with fear and trembling" (Philippians 2:12). The Christian life is a life of progression, but can alternatively become a falling away. The Christian knight I encountered in my vision of hell had fallen from a high place and his soul had become lost. There are Christians in purgatory in the Spirit realm, and by that I mean that this life here is itself a purgation, as well it must be, or there is no inner life of the Spirit, no redemption of the soul. Cheap grace happens for no one.

Atonement, however, is happening forever within Divine being, and thus it is through moment-by-moment grace that we are finally liberated from sin, from the deep karmic bondage that determines our lives. It is through this agency of mercy that we avoid the face of judgment and enter into heaven outside the restricting parameters of our own purity and merit alone, while also including them, because in seeing us God sees his own mercy, the effects of his agency, in which we participate and for which we too, are responsible. This will become more clear later when we explore redemption on the Path of the Son.

We are redeemed to redeem on the scale of our grace and merit in this and other lives, and our task as all humans is to heal the world. Christ set the example that we are intended to follow, and it is in this path that there is grace. Christianity is the way of the Cross, and in this way, grace is earned in its fulfillment.

In short, there is work to be done!

Chapter 11

Archangels Uriel and Michael

In this chapter I will share the final piece of background for part three, which is the groundwork for the following theology. As with other personal spiritual experiences that I have shared, for many of you it will be helpful to simply understand my experiences as internal processes which are being used to illustrate important points about Crisis and Transformation, whether they be dreams, visions, or spiritual encounters. What is important, is that they can be useful.

After living five months on Green Gulch Farm Community I left and was doing some manual work for a contractor putting down cement. When I was working one day, I was feeling angry about how another employee was being treated, and in this state of heightened awareness I heard a voice in my head, "My name is Uriel." I eventually went home and looked this up. Uriel is an Archangel. And so I inquired in meditation a few days later, "what does this mean? Why did I hear this?" I was then told to open up the Bible, and I opened to a place in Psalms where it says "to break the arms of the wicked" (Psalms 10:15). Then I was told that Uriel had difficult and sometimes dark tasking but that he had another side, which was Ariel and that this side was a catalyst for creative endeavor.

Mystified by this experience, after some research I contacted a Rabbi to try to make sense of what was going on. The Rabbi confirmed that my experience was meaningful, informing me that each Archangel had a converse aspect and that Oriel was yet another side of Uriel.

After having done some further study I was given a book on Uriel by the current Vatican angelologist, Don Marcello Stanzione, called, "Uriel, the Disappeared Archangel." According to the Jesuit theologians cited in this book, Uriel is directly associated with the Holy Spirit, and although no longer venerated in the Catholic church, Archangel Uriel continues to be venerated in all Orthodox churches.

One of the great Protestant mystics, Jakob Böhme, also associated Uriel with the Holy Spirit. Archangel Uriel as Ariel has additionally figured in highest initiations of the Scottish Rite and is similarly centrally important in the Rosicrucian tradition, which also derives from Protestantism. We first see Archangel Uriel in the Book of Enoch, a 3rd century BCE text used by early church fathers and from which Christ quotes in the Book of Jude. Uriel similarly figures importantly in the Enochic tradition of Jewish mysticism. Therefore, I associate Uriel with the Path of the Spirit, which is consistent with the Jesuit interpretation, and also with Kabbalism, as well as with my own experiences.

A few months after I had finished the construction job, I also had a dream in which

I first saw a glowing shade of orange; I felt the presence of Archangel Michael; and I then saw the figures of men sitting meditation around an orb. Though I had never before been there, I knew that they were in Tallinn, the capital of Estonia, and felt drawn –guided– toward the city and the scene that in my dream I'd seen. And then, the dream was over and I awoke.

It was clear to me that this was a Divine calling and as I was fortunate enough to be able to do so, I resolved immediately to embark upon a journey to the city of Tallinn.

- *Marcello Stanzione. Carmine Alvino. Urielè: L'Arcangelo Scomparso. SugarCo: 2017.*
- *Margaret Barker. The Lost Prophet: The Book of Enoch and its Influence on Christianity. Sheffield Phoenix Press: 2005.*
- *Antoine Faivre. Western Esotericism: A Concise History. New York: SUNY Press, 2015.*

PART III. New Knowledge

Introduction

In part three, we will look at the *Path of Trinity*, a theology that can revolutionize how Christianity is lived today by opening up space for— and showing the necessity of— dedicated spiritual practice and inner processes of psychological health.

This will be a potentially challenging part, for what I hope to illuminate is complicated and something that constantly challenges my understanding of it as I evolve. I am confident that as we explore these themes together, it will be also be profoundly rewarding. What is revealed is theology, which when used in practical application, solves the psychic split in Christianity that has caused so many problems at the level of the individual, and as a tradition. In the context of this, we will look at imperfect divinization, that is, reaching a highest spiritual level without true perfection.

We will also see how theological divides between two of the major Christian traditions, Catholicism and Orthodoxy, can be resolved. To anticipate, this will require defining the difference between knowable and unknowable God and solving the so-called filioque clause though a *Spirit-centric trinitarianism that goes back to pre-trinitarian Christian concepts of God*. The understanding that follows from this is *consistent with proto-orthodox precursors of contemporary Christian theology* as we have it today. I will also, towards concluding, look at the Divine Feminine in terms of agency.

Chapter 12

Following Paths

Later, in Tallinn Estonia...

I went and sat meditation there with the Zen people and explored the city. I found the Orthodox church and went inside where I met a priest and asked him if he had an icon of Archangel Michael. He then took me to an icon that was illuminated with candles and was black, except for the orange-hued sash around the waist of this Archangel, like the color I had seen in my dream. (I would later associate Archangel Michael with the Path of the Son).

This was confirmation. I was on the right track. The many promptings that I had, which promised me reward for going to this far-away land, had been clearly sensed and were being validated in the external world. And, it was on a train up from the Russian border near Värska and the Pskovo-Pechersky Monastery, that I received the theological framework for the Paths of the Trinity which follows.

What are the Paths of the Trinity?

There are three Paths from which we can choose, each of which relates to, and extend from, the Trinity. Something fundamental is implied here, which is firstly that nothing is separate, no one Path excludes the other, and each is only in balance, in harmony, when taken with the other. And the key to understanding this relationship, as we know from Part II above, is that indeed of all relating at the deeper level, is the felt experience, the conscious discipline, of being-in-relationship. Through the Trinity we become into ultimate being-in-relationship.

Few people realize that it was not until the council of Nicea in the 4th century that the concept of the Trinity was fully concluded and that many in the early church saw the Trinity as being faces of God, as we saw earlier in our observations of how early Christians in the Merkabah tradition conceptualized the front and back of God in visions. In fact, it took many years and many different doctrines for the idea of the Trinity to find its now most commonly used formulation.

While this in no way suggests that this formalism is untrue, still, because of this, it is essential that we —as in the case of looking at the Biblical texts themselves— hold this with an open regard. We must come back to this age-old story with the eyes of the early Christians, with a willingness to see God in different forms of agency beyond the specific dynamism of the Trinity, particularly in its current theological renderings, which are still a matter of ongoing dispute among Christianity's traditions.

Before the Trinity became church dogma, many of the earliest Christians, who were in the tradition that is now almost universally accepted by the church, did not conceive of God as a thing, but as *energies*, and in this respect they considered Christ to be God's agency for redemption (p. 50 CCT). This is notably true of the Christians in 1st century Merkabah tradition since they saw Christ as the back of God, as God's Mercy. It will be essential to keep this in mind as we explore the Paths of the Trinity.

- *Peter C. Phan, ed. Cambridge Companion to The Trinity. Cambridge: Cambridge University Press, 2011.*

Chapter 13

The Path of the Father

Judgment and Power - Creation and Destruction

The Path of the Father first appears with Genesis where God walks with Adam in the Garden. This is a Path of obedience, of submission and surrender to the Divine Will. The most memorable of these relationships is perhaps Abraham, who receives a direct visitation from God. He then enters into a relationship with the Father and is asked to sacrifice his only son, Isaac. He obeys, but a lamb is provided. In the Jewish tradition, there is an alternate telling where the lamb is not provided, and Isaac is sacrificed.

The radical and emotionally horrific nature of Abraham's path in these moments required what Kierkegaard called "faith by virtue of the absurd," that is, an obedience beyond the pale of reason and moral logic. Without absurdity, "Abraham is lost." (Fear and Trembling). Another example may be Christ's plea in the Garden of Gethsemane. He begins in agony, praying for the cup of his suffering to pass over, but then resolves into a kind of Kierkegaardian "absurd" obedience, an acquiescence into God's will. This is being-in-relationship with the Father.

The Path of the Father is not easy. It is demanding, and can easily be terrifying, and always involves and evokes a *mysterium tremendum*, the sublime (in the Kantian sense), the fear of the absolute and radical Divine Other (Rudolph Otto). The Law of the Father is harsh, and disobedience is said to result in certain death, as the Israelites learned in the Desert. On the other hand, obedience empowers. The powers of the world and of the Spirit arise from the Path of the Father and continue to follow it. The risks, the fallen states of this Path, are a turning to disobedience, becoming truly evil, being guilty of the sin of Satan, or, of using power to appropriate without being-in-relationship, without being in the Harmony of the Trinity. Solomon fell into this trap. The specific sense of sin given by the Greek word used in the Septuagint to translate what we read as "sin," is, *tolma*, "willfulness," and similarly expresses this trap.

There is a wrong way to walk this Path, which leads to ossification and legalism, a reversion to a slavish obedience of the rules *to the letter* and for their own sake, accepting only authoritative interpretations of the written Torah alone without living the life of the Spirit. In Spiritual terms, this is a mode of a soul-death, living in a fixed and structured system, unable to adapt. Most western faith traditions embody this flawed version of spiritual practice, or some form of this lack of true dedication and mindfulness, and this includes much of Christianity today.

However, the obedient exercise of spiritual rules and practices, committed in obedience to the law of the Father and to the honor of God, in harmony with the Spirit, can result in the virtues and enlightenment which can be found in the Christian monastic traditions and in Orthodox Judaism. All of these represent the Path of the Father. In the Old Testament, Job, David, and Abraham took this Path.

Chapter 14

The Path of the Spirit: An Introduction

The reason I have chosen to share the very unique travel narrative in this Chapter, is that it illustrates the interconnectedness of all life, which is essential to understand in order to follow the Path of the Spirit. We are all in this together, in both our everyday reality and also in the spiritual dimension. Contemporary science and quantum physics are starting to make this more known for the rational mind, but the following story illustrates how this can practically and naturally occur within the limitations of human consciousness.

When we set an intention with high levels of concentration in a heightened spiritual state there can be long-lasting effects that can shift the natural flow of reality which is otherwise very bound by causal determinism. Indeed it is bound, despite our collective illusion that we have a great variety of choices. In the physical realm, we are limited by preconditioned options, but if we operate spiritually miracles can happen that translate even to the physical realm. Christ was not speaking merely metaphorically when he said that faith could move mountains. The reality we imagine to be fixed is more fluid, more interconnected than we realize.

Years ago, as a young missionary, I went to work along the Amazon tributaries of the Guyanese interior with the Amerindian Indians. This was the first time I experienced the powerful potential effects of shamanic practices. In one village the chief, who was known as a powerful shaman, had welcomed me in but during my visit proposed to me that I marry either of his daughters, which I declined to do. This made him angry and was a humiliation, despite my not intending this, and the villagers came to me secretly later that day to tell me to leave, that he was putting a curse on me.

There are essentially two kinds of shamanism, dark shamanism, based in judgment and which loosely correlates to the gift of prophecy, and white shamanism, based in mercy, which corresponds to the gift of healing and clairvoyance. There is a whole range of these different skills, but this shaman was a dark shaman.

I immediately got very sick and despite my spiritual practices found that all I could do was pray. To counteract this kind of attack directly and immediately it requires highly developed spiritual skills that only come as a result of deep meditation and prayer if they are not a natural gift. In this case, prayer and scripture-reading were my only recourse, and I survived the attack. However, for many months after leaving the Amazon, I would every morning have an illness that came from this experience. But not only did I have that, I also experienced a terrible thorn in the flesh that I now associate directly with the effects of my refusal, and his subsequent curse. Few people, especially contemporary Christians, will be able to understand this. But I am not alone in my experience of the Guyanese interior. I later learned that an American professor of anthropology, Neil Whitehead, died of an unknown illness, which he associated with a spiritual attack in this very jungle.

It was almost exactly twenty years later that I was delivered from this, after months of struggle following my awakening and slow return to Christianity. In a dream, a woman, a Siberian shaman, did a ritual and made the sign of the Cross. It was a Siberian shaman who took away the curse of an Amazonian shaman with the sign of the Cross in the four directions. I don't completely understand this experience, or why she presented in this way, but I can say that after twenty years it is a fact that I am freed. And for this am extremely grateful. So much so that I subsequently got a visa and secured a teaching job on the Mongolian steppes near Siberia, hoping to possibly meet her. I finally did not do this and did not meet the woman whose work in the spirit realm had freed me, who I suspect is no longer living.

That said, one of my practices is to ask Archangel Michael for help when there are spiritual intrusions of the kind I experienced in Guyana, along with some other tools that I will share later. The practices of dark shamanism are to be avoided and in this way one does not cause harm. To do otherwise perpetuates evil in the spirit realm and has very negative results here too, eventually coming back on the person who did it, either in this world or the next. An awakened person should never use empowerment to produce pain or destruction and has to guard against doing this themselves by holding onto anger or fear.

An experience with Shamanism may not quite resonate with you, but what is crucial to understand in this context, is the difference between the Spirit-filled life and the spirits-filled life. You must learn to "test the spirits to see what sort they are" (1 John 4:1) and maintain your integrity. Just like in choosing friends here in our ordinary reality, it is important to be wise and aware. Eventually, you will recognize and appreciate the angels and those who have gone before who are helping you. You should not search out spirits for help but always ask for guidance from God and your guardian angel. Mediumship, which is intentionally searching out unfamiliar spirits, is a practice that should be avoided, though some awakened persons will experience this naturally, as I have described above. This is understandable, because this is what it is to be part of the larger reality. It is just the way it *actually* is.

In a similar vein, some angels are considered dark angels but even these are there to test and try you, and God allows this. In the Buddhist tradition, it is suggested that you "feed your demons;" this may sound shocking to a Christian, but this is because what you offer in this kind of nurturing, is a kindness to all beings, and so you should not operate from a place of fear but with "power and of love and of a sound mind" (2 Timothy 1:7). True evil cannot stand to be in the presence of love, and will go away. This is the core thing to understand in dealing with this. Put on the armor of God by "standing in truth, righteousness, peace, and faith, praying always with all prayer and supplication in the Spirit" (Ephesians 6:11-18).

When you operate in fear, you fall into delusions and attract evil. Pam Coronado, former president of the International Remote Viewers Association, once told me, "Travis, it is like AM and FM radio. The pain and trauma, the negative, is the stronger signal. I can walk down a street where a murder occurred twenty years ago, and this is the strongest signal that comes to me, not all the years of happy children playing." She also gave me some other related good advice, "Control your gift, don't let your gift control you." In other words, don't be drawn into pain and darkness, see it if it is there and let it go, control what comes to you, not the other way around. In the darkness is no end of delusion and deluded spirits (Ephesians 6:12). Your light, and your faith is sufficient to penetrate the darkness and bring life. Also, *don't look for darkness where there is none*. Life is intricate and beautiful, not something to be feared.

Now, all these years later, I found myself on Muhu Island in Estonia ..

Muhu is the epicenter of natural religion in Estonia. Muhu is a tiny island, and I was staying with very kind hosts on their sheep farms. While there I had a warm visit with a friend of theirs, the island expert on Maausk, Estonia's pre-Christian native faith. We stood with him at the Ilmapuu, the native tree, and observed his approach to natural energies. Natural religion has been influential in the Christian tradition, notably among the Celtic Christians, and it is integral to my practice, to my experience of the world as interconnected. This understanding of the unique properties, spiritual qualities and energies of places, objects and animal life is a fundamental truth. The Christian Orthodox faith, which still exists on the island, also holds this view as part of their inner tradition and experience of the Divine in nature.

One morning at 5am I woke up and realized that there was a presence outside my island hut and that it was communicating with me. I looked out my window to the pole in the yard and did not know what it was, except that it was intense. It asked very simply and directly, "are you coming out? -decide" -and I thought a bit and said, "no," since I had no reason to go out and had just been woken. Then the presence left. A minute or two later I heard the sheep running hard in the pasture and so I went outside my hut to see what was going on. They had been split into two groups and were running in a panic. It was the wolf; he got one. A nearby farmer finally killed the wolf. He had come over from the mainland during the sea freeze the year before.

Shortly after this, when I returned home to East Tennessee, I had a dream where I saw a cow out in a pasture that I knew was sick. The next day I saw this cow. I did

73

not know what was wrong, and so I walked out into the field with a bowl of water, and when I got to her, she had blood and mucus coming out of her nose. I offered her water and she showed me her legs and that she could still stand and told me she was still strong, and so I contacted the farmer and let him know. I have had this kind of experience a few times since I was a child —excepting one instance some years back where a stray cat simply came to me for help to save her litter, and guided me to them— but in all these cases there were important issues the animals were experiencing, and their needs were perceivable to me.

In conclusion, following from these illustrations, we can see that we are connected to all the world around us, but we often don't realize it, and awakening to this is an important part of living the life of the Spirit. In Estonia, despite this being one of the most technologically advanced countries in Europe, there are still wood fires burning in the homes, still natural simplicity, and therefore, a lingering, ancient, and deep connection to nature. The life of the Spirit is acknowledged, and unsurprisingly, this then presents in human consciousness. This Life is all around us, we just have to awaken into it.

Chapter 15

Farther Down the Path: Authenticity and Harmony

Thus far, we have already encountered the Path of Spirit in small ways, anticipating a fuller presentation of the concept as not just a theory, but an integrated form of theological praxis. We have seen that the Path of the Spirit is concerned with all Life; it penetrates and sustains all Life, it is in both the sacred and the profane. The Spirit is involved in all spiritually-heightening practices. To put it in more southern language, the Spirit is *down and dirty*, produces wholeness out of fractured reality and liberates us from karmic bondage. The Spirit also allows for shadow integration, a harmonizing of the self, as well as self-purification through recognizing and addressing that which we do not wish to be. Thus, as we will see in this section, harmony and authenticity are the result of this Path.

The risk on the Path of the Spirit is to assume you can become (to put in plain language) a free-wheeling spiritual "do-it-yourself dude," i.e., the awakened agnostic, the spiritual atheist or even a nihilist who would cultivate the empty field without affirming life. More philosophically, I mean to suggest that the risk is of individuation and awakening without being-in-relationship, of self-realization without surrender to the Father. The risk is a Nietzschean overman, the so-called spiritually-enlightened person who is not in the harmony of the Trinity. As we explore the Path from the perspective of harmony and authenticity together, I hope to compel you to avoid these risks.

To begin, we must consider the Fruits of the Spirit. These, namely, "love, joy, peace, patience, kindness, goodness, faithfulness, gentleness, and self-control," only manifest through ongoing works of grace, realized in choice and action. Thus to any realization of "Spirit," we add the word "Path." It is critical to do the walking, or, to put it another way, right belief, or orthodoxy, is only as good as the good and righteous deeds it inspires: ortho*praxy*. In short, there is work to be done! One must purify one's heart and mind. The Celtic Christian mystics called the Holy Spirit "the Wild Goose," as you will be taken in every direction needed to do this, namely, to unlock your Soul's code. By "code" we might simply consider that the Spirit is multifaceted, and embodies infinite energies, including our own.

This resonates, to my mind, with the diversity of Spirit that is mentioned in Isaiah: "The Spirit of the LORD shall rest upon him, the Spirit of wisdom and understanding, the Spirit of counsel and might, the Spirit of knowledge and of the fear of the LORD, and He will delight in the fear of the Lord" (Isaiah 11:2).

The early Christians did not believe in the Spirit as a person (CCT p. 50), and rightly so as the Spirit is the Divine in everything, the Divine unknowable undergirding G-d's agencies, and most importantly the throne of God. (To creatively, perhaps playfully demonstrate this as I write, allow me to sometimes invoke "G-d" as a formulation —also used in Judaism— that signifies "God" as unknowable being, and sometimes to write "God," signifying a being that can be experienced directly through gnosis, or apophatic knowledge).

We are all embodying in Spirit that essence of G-d that animates the entire world, expressing both the masculine and feminine principles in interiority, that is, the principles of judgment/creation and love/mercy. In the Godself, in the experienceable Soul of unknowable G-d, Spirit is the gifting of life. *The Spirit is thus not one specific agency. It is instead general; it is a plenitude of agency from which follow other members in terms of their specific agency*, and is only as such a member of the formalism of the Trinity. The aspects of judgment and creation, as are expressed in the Father, and lastly, mercy and self-sacrifice, as expressed through the Son, are active and experienceable agency, also expressions of Spirit.

Understood in this way, an important Catholic-Orthodox divide is solved, both the *filioque clause* and also the problem of experienceable God versus unknowable G-d. The clause or controversy I am referring to is an ancient one that separates these two major branches of the church. It is a question of whether or not the Holy Spirit proceeds, that is comes out from, the Father, or the Father *and* the Son. Effectively, *how* does the Holy Spirit come to be? After thousands of years theologians are still stumped on this one, still in disagreement, over which is more natural, especially since they created this quandary themselves. It has actually caused real division and suffering.

Based on my study of the early church I understand and experience the Trinity in a completely different way that resolves this otherwise irreconcilable problem. To my mind, the Holy Spirit undergirds and animates all the essential life energies, including the agency of the Trinity, whilst it is also neither but is rather co-continuous, and thus the Spirit of Christ is also the Spirit of God. *A paradox therefore remains, but not a controversy.*

However, it is important to add that *the agency of the Father and of the Son are experienceable expressions of unknowable G-d, understood also as Spirit, or Ein Sof,* in the Jewish Mystical tradition, the foundation being, an unknowable essence. Seen in this way, *the formalism of the Trinity expresses the Logos of G-d, the Word of G-d, the Truth of G-d, is the knowable from the unknowable, Soul of God from Spirit of G-d; the true formalism of the Trinity is therefore how G-d expresses ultimate being to us and through us and is beyond time.*

Indeed, Wisdom ("Sophia" in Greek) is rightly also personified as Spirit, as the Feminine Divine. As we have seen, the Trinity is itself is the Truth of G-d, and therefore realizes Wisdom throughout its infinite agencies. "The beginning of wisdom is this: Get wisdom. Though it cost all you have, get understanding. Cherish her, and she will exalt you; embrace her, and she will honor you. She will give you a garland to grace your head and present you with a glorious crown" (Proverbs 4:5-9). Sophia presents to me in nature as an owl, although she is usually depicted as a woman in Christian icons.

In the Jewish mystical tradition there is an understanding of an upper Sophia and a lower Sophia, which can be linked to the *Shekhinah*, the Feminine exiled Glory of God. The Christian Gnostic tradition also sees Sophia as in some sense fallen, and in both traditions this can be understood by realizing that Wisdom is a lower level —a functional level— of non-rational Truth that is beyond time, or upper Sophia as is understood in Judaism. A prayer that acknowledges Wisdom as an aspect of the Shekhinah and invites guidance and protection, is a Jewish children's prayer that is prayed before bedtime and which I recommend praying regularly, "May Michael be at my right, Gabriel at my left, Uriel in front of me,

Raphael behind me, and above my head, the Shekhinah—the Divine Presence."

Although I will not expand upon this in depth here, it may be noted that the Path of the Spirit is not without kinship across cultures. Very briefly, we might nod to the resonant Path of the Spirit in the spiritual tradition of the Sioux tribes, and in applications of Christian Kabbalah and the paths of the Sefirot. Another resonance is found in the East, where the Path of the Spirit is perhaps best represented by Taoism. Some might hold that the three non-theistic religions of the East, Confucianism (Father), Taoism (Spirit), and Buddhism (Son) follow in similar sequence historically and are the *via negativa* to the *via positiva* of the West, which results in direct relationship with God.

In all of these glimpses of various interpretations of the wisdom of the paths at hand, we have already observed anticipations of the Path of the Son. We will develop this Path below. Our main focus in this chapter has been the path of the Spirit; another is the path of the Father. These should not cause unnecessary confusion, but are simply other ways we can think of the work that is to be done to be-in-relation with God.

Falling Upwards 1: The Need to be Broken

We're running up the hill through the Way of the Cross like mad, my mother running along with me. We had just been down to the creek and got into pods of chiggers, the bane of any hiker —or unwitting penitent— in the Ozarks. Back at Assumption Abbey we went to our rooms and began to scrape them off, trying to do so in time to make the afternoon mass with the monks. It would take months before the itching agony stopped, but as a local hillbilly myself I well understood the costs in advance. This Trappist monastery in my hometown of Ava Missouri would be the first in two monastery stays we would do together in this— the last year of my awakening. Considering what would come in the months ahead, the long-lasting oozing chigger bites were nothing.

True transformation and death-in-life is painful, if often necessary. It may be compared to a complete tearing apart as the potter remakes the vessel. This can happen at any point in spiritual ascent. Like an egg re-becoming over and over again, or like a Phoenix that immolates and then rises from the ashes, I had gone through a number of death-in-life experiences along the way of my transformation, but what would happen next would be unlike anything I had experienced before, a psychological collapse that has lasted exactly a year until now and went far beyond the "rock bottom" that I experienced in France. It is only now that I am finally able to write about what happened. This experience left me an utterly changed man, a man who fell, but who fell upwards.

I had started on the Path of the Father, but not the path of following a specific tradition. I allowed myself to be awakened into direct obedience, which can be very scary and will invariably result in the fear of the Lord. When I was prompted to go to Estonia I went, and as a result received Paths of the Trinity. Following also the Path of the Spirit, I had awakening and was shining the light inwardly and living in uncompromising truth, which had also produced clarity of vision and internal purity.

That said, what had resulted from this was very much my own spiritual DNA in action and as such was not wholly transformed into perfection despite my level of ascent. In Taoist terms, I was still only embodying my personal *Chi*. I was advanced, but still functioning without consistently holding the mind of Christ.

My soul had been purified, and I had ascended to an important point, but the completed fruits of the spirit were still lacking. In my climb on the ladder of divine ascent I had arisen through wisdom without having in equal balance love. I had been a bit like a man hopping up on one leg. Love without wisdom can be useless, but I wasn't merely useless, I was actually spiritually dangerous; I was spiritually empowered but still lacking in the most essential of the fruits of the Spirit, *Love.*

With Saint Pio as my spiritual guide, there was no way to go but down. I had to fall and to be broken in order to follow in Christ's steps entirely and to enter into the fullest harmony of the Trinity. To reach the self-emptying that is necessary to open onto the Path of the Son fully: to walk the *Path of the Heart.*

Chapter 16

The Path of the Son

Love and Mercy, Redemption and Completion

The Path of the Son is self-sacrificing compassion and involves living a life of unconditional love. This is a radical path of giving, of existence entirely for-another, and of prizing the heavenly rewards due to all those who follow this path over all profane pleasures or properties.

Christ was very clear about what this Path entails, which is taking up one's cross and denying himself and following Christ (Matthew 16:24-26). Modeled in the early church, this took form as a communal style of life, a community in which each received from others in the community in accordance with his needs; the loving openness and passivity with which they received their enemies; and finally, a resolute willingness to give their own lives as martyrs to the faith, rather than resisting the abuses and oppression of persecutors and enemies.

Unsurprisingly, it is difficult to have a family and follow this path in exclusivity as Saint Paul rightly observed. You risk losing everything, including your family. Another risk is becoming inauthentic. A person who is not whole (Spirit) or wholly surrendered (Father) will not be able to sustain this Path outside of a supportive community. This finally results in the highest form of completion and mastery, but it happens beyond the narrow constraints of personal ego or temporal concerns.

There must be a death to self and a giving of all for others, a becoming into complete expression of love and mercy. Christianity itself is thus the feminine expression of the Divine as it is based in mercy and compassion, rather than power and judgment, which is correctly associated with the Father. As such, both the Theotokos, that is Mary, and Christ are an expression of the Divine Feminine! The image of Mary holding Christ is also an expression of the cross, is a precursor to Mary's pathos at the foot of the Cross. *Christianity is therefore the feminine expression of monotheism.*

Christ and Mary are embodied expressions of the aspect of God which is love made flesh in a real person, as perfect expression of mercy in human agency. It is through this agency of mercy that we avoid the face of judgment and enter into heaven outside the restricting parameters of our purity and merit alone, while also necessarily including them. This is because in seeing us God sees his mercy, that is, the effect of his agency, in which we also participate and for which we are responsible.

At the outset of this Chapter, we anticipated that grace would play a key role in explicating the Paths. Now, taking the perspective of the Path of the Son, we are in a position to grasp that purpose, as we observe that mix of agencies which is both our own and God's. Christ set the example that we are intended to follow and it is on this Path that there is grace. There are no shortcuts, and it is only by incredible grace that you can remain there.

However, standing in this redemption requires alignment, and effort. For *although God's judgment is mediated by mercy, through divine co-suffering, we must intentionally and unceasingly align ourselves with the image of Christ, with perfect personhood. This is the best metaphor of grace and effort.* To become Christ, to enter into *theosis*, is finally to fully enter into this complete self-emptying in love, that is to say that we are redeemed to redeem, and it is only in being in the image of Christ that we are completely perfected in love. I will, however, suggest that we neither take this notion of "perfection" too lightly, nor too literally.

That I saw the back of God in the vision that I shared at the beginning is understandable when explained in this way. Direct relationship with God, as we saw earlier, can involve fear and trembling because God turns his face of judgment in our direction. This is why it is said that no one can see the face of God and live. *Christ is the physical embodiment of Divine mercy, and is metaphorically a turning away of the Divine face of judgment.*

We must have absolute faith in Divine Providence. But this faith truly experienced understands that without effort we can become alienated and fall from grace. We must "work out our salvation with fear and trembling" (Philippians 2:12). As I have tried to suggest in multiple ways above, there is a reality regarding the concept of hell and there is indeed an intelligible way to conceive of the transmigration of souls, but to *focus on this,* is to fall. So stand in faith. "Without faith, it is impossible to please God because anyone who comes to him must believe that he exists and that he rewards those who earnestly seek him" (Hebrews 11:6).

Only through the empowerment of the Spirit, through the harmony of the Trinity, can the Path of the Son be realized in authenticity, in obedience to the Father. The Path of the Son is pure love. Here there is neither negativity nor nothingness, but living truth. This is the Path of Christ and of the Saints.

Falling Upwards 2: Being Broken

Some months after leaving the monasteries I began to fall sick. I had been told in a vision that the Spirit would leave me and that my spiritual DNA would be set back, and I knew there would be a "going down" of some kind, such as the days of illness I remembered from the experience of going to hell. Some weeks after this, in October of 2016, I became very ill and was not even able to leave my room, I was under so much torment. I prayed the Lord's Prayer for hours, sometimes to the point of exhaustion, and finally I had a response, that I should pray "Not my Will But Thine Be Done." I did, and then went into a vision.

In the vision, I saw Saint Pio in a great golden church facing forward to the front, and I saw behind him a daemon, a presence, a flawed being upon a throne, which he seemed to be aware of but was doing nothing about, and so I immediately rose from my place below and began making the sign of the cross, going directly toward this entity. But then I went into a place where three brutish men came to beat me and I was thrown into a state of the worst possible accusations someone could make on my life, which were untrue, but had at some time in the past had a true potential. Then I went into a great suffering. It became so great that I spontaneously wished for the end of my own life and that of the world itself, which felt like a great and unnecessary suffering. Finally, I found myself above and in front of the enthroned but flawed entity toward whom I had made the sign of the cross. And behind me were other great beings supporting me, including one who had come to my aid. Upon seeing us, the flawed being on his throne cut one of his arms off, then, with some reticence, I cut off the other one. I was floating like cherubim during this time and found myself again in the grand church with Saint Pio.

He then moved from his place in the church and guided me to stand there. At this point I suddenly became covered in golden armor that had such a great weight upon my otherwise naturally suspended state that I wanted away from the burden and so then found myself floating above Padre Pio, head to head with him, seen as a cherub, saying the Lord's Prayer, and then "Not My Will But Thine Be Done." I felt a release from a mission, or a surrendering of it to God. As I left and came back into my body I heard the Protestant gospel song, "there's a new name written down in glory, and it's mine..."

Immediately I felt well enough to leave my room and so I did, and suggested that someone take me for a drive. However, just one mile from leaving we came upon a dead dog just killed in the road, with his fellow canine companion just standing there, not knowing what to do. In the very moment I saw them I broke into tears, knowing that somehow, somewhere, I had lost someone, and in that very moment, I collapsed into incoherence. I had entered into deep suffering and mental anguish. What I had become was completely broken.

What can we learn from this?

I believe the being toward which I made the sign of the cross, the flawed one upon his throne, becoming into deification but having only two golden arms, was actually my archetype, my imperfect divinization in Spirit. I had come that far but had not been purified. So to become into the perfect image of Christ I had to be defeated, and had done that myself with help. Every human who emerges in imperfection, who does not dwell in perfect love and compassion, will be eventually be defeated, in this world or the next. What happened to me was the result of imperfect divinization.

However, I got broken in the right way, in the way that one should be, in the way to start again with a mind brought into captivity, into the mind of Christ, surrendered to this calling of self-sacrifice and care. I hope this experience will help you to realize that walking the Path of the Spirit and following the will of the Father without fully entering into compassion, will result in defeat, in this world or the next. You must enter fully into the harmony of the Trinity by living in *love*. Of the fruits of the Spirit, the "greatest of these is love." *All Paths must embody each other in relationship.*

Summary of Paths of the Trinity

The Paths of the Trinity progressively mirror the personal development of a human from youth to old age— of our potential progress as spiritual beings— and also it might be argued that of God and man together in the course of human history. As such also it might be said that we are moving from the Power and Judgment phase (Father) to the Harmony and Self-Realizing phase (Spirit), to finally the Love and Self-Sacrifice (Son), where the Self-Sacrificing Love of Christ becomes our shared reality.

In terms of Palamist or neo-Palamist Christianity, that is to say, in the mystical tradition of the Eastern Orthodox churches, these Paths reflect and embody the ternary structure of the contemplative practice that leads from *catharsis to theoria*, and from *theoria to theosis*, the transformative process whose aim is likeness to or union with God. In the Protestant Conservative Holiness tradition which emerged from 19th-century Methodism, this is similarly reflected in the movement from *salvation to sanctification, to entire sanctification*. We will briefly discuss these stages and processes in the next section.

PART IV. Interiority and Practice Disciplines

Introduction

In part three we looked at the core theological underpinnings that will support this next section, which deals with the Trinity as a form of interiority. By "form of interiority" I mean here, an in-depth spiritual process that involves but finally goes beyond that which is characterized by sensibility and affectivity, that is to say it goes beyond that which includes motivations and experiences that are purely rational or emotional. Here we are looking at what it means to go deep into spiritual transformation, through following these paths. In this part we will revisit awakening and ascent and give methods to achieve and maintain psychological health during this process. We will look at practical issues and propose workable solutions related to inner experience.

Chapter 17

Obedience and Surrender

Walking the Path of the Father

To follow the Path of the Father, you must first submit yourself to a spiritual tradition. In the Old Testament, the way humanity experienced God was through the requirement of obedience and though judgment that had its effects in the physical realm and which often concerned the practical life of the people, including moral law. This is the way God first revealed himself and it is similarly thus with the individual. It is related to how we must behave and what we must do in this earthly life to be honorable and righteous.

Within spiritual traditions we are given forms to follow and rules of conduct that allow us to connect with God in this way. It allows us to follow codes that preserve the integrity of and protect the physical lives of nations and peoples by following structures of morality. To enter into internal processes that reflect this, we must come into humility and obedience. Some spiritual traditions are toxic, and every faith practice is potentially flawed, so it becomes also a matter of personal discernment as to whether or not you should commit to a tradition, and this becomes especially important when it comes to discerning the character of those who you might allow to guide you. Too many have had their souls damaged by unhealthy religion, which is why this path holds considerable risk, even as it is necessary and affords stability.

That said, following a tradition and obeying its forms and moral content with high levels of intention toward detail —with a spirit of concentration and effort— is an effective interior process. Every act of obedience in this way generates merit, and if done authentically and in a spirit of humility, can lead to awakening. This is not a descent into obsessive-compulsive behavior, but it has something of this quality because it understands that acts of intended positivity and honor toward God's laws energetically produce a gifting toward all those around you, and therefore, back to yourself. Every gift has an equal or greater return.

These are levels of intention that most people do not carry out in their daily lives, but it is possible to live in sustained internal obedience without following highly prescribed monastic rules such as that of the Cistercian order, or other highly-defined traditions such as Hasidism. While living in Manchester England I sometimes visited a Chabad house, a Hasidic Jewish household, and along with my studies watched meal preparation. While observing what was required, such as food selection, hand washing and prayer, I had the natural realization of how even seemingly minute gestures can be made consciously to God's glory. Regardless of your tradition, you can enter into similar practices, or even invent them yourself. Find an internal discipline that you can externalize and that works for you.

What is important to understand is that every act matters and can be internally purifying. If you hold consistently in mind that every act and intention matter, and are to be done to the glory of God, and do this with a high level of consciousness, you will have actualized the most important underlying discipline of this practice. Every turn of your consciousness, every gesture, is a spiritual movement that has immediate ripple effects, both within yourself and toward those around you, and impacts the world at large.

For the person who is awakened in Spirit, this may result in the higher application of this path, which follows from awakened surrender and listening to God and may even require going precisely beyond these moral codes themselves into direct obedience. By "direct obedience" I mean, a non-rational, but intentional surrender which lives in fear of the Lord. You even may be required to go to a foreign land, or to give up something you hold dear. You will be tested internally to the point of breaking.

However, the resulting gifts of God that follow from this are judgment, wisdom and discernment. You will have shed the traditional structures that are only the outer garment of relationship with God, while also functioning within them. Realized internally, this is judgment and creation; it is wisdom that finally has to be balanced with love to climb the ladder of Divine ascent. This is the face of God that we don't get to see. And for good reason.

The prayer that I suggest to pray many times over to internalize this obedience and open up the path to direct relationship is the one Jesus taught, prayed in entirety, *"Our father who art in heaven hallowed be thy name ..."* Remember that this is included: "and lead us not into temptation but deliver us from evil." God will send his angels to test you and will often allow you to fail, in order to learn. These will finally be errors that can be redeemed so long as you stay obedient.

If the angelic testing gets too great —you most certainly will be direly tried as your dedication is tested— call out *"Elohim Adonai."* But don't do it unless you really need help. This plea for help works in other crisis situations as well, but must only be used when the situation is desperate, where there is no longer something to be learned or where an outcome risks becoming evil.

Realized internally, this will result in what in the Christian Orthodox Contemplative tradition is *catharsis*, the purification of mind and body. This is also known in the Protestant Holiness tradition as *salvation*, an initial work of grace that leads to *sanctification*, or purification. This is a common expression in Protestant Christianity, to be "saved" or to be "born again."

However, being "born again" in the Christian esoteric tradition— in the inner teachings of Christianity for which the formal church is the outer garments— has a deeper meaning (John 3:1-21). It is about a deep awakening into true reality, to firstly be "born of water" which is to come into harmony with nature and to awaken to the true self. Here we again encounter a resonance with Taoism, in the notion of the water path. Briefly, this entails being born into the flow of reality at a higher level of consciousness, and moving within this, something we discussed earlier concerning my own experience of awakening. This connection with the eastern tradition finds a unique difference however, if we consider that this idea of being born again also means to be "born of Spirit," which is to begin to become one with the God's will, which is different than fully embodying your personal *Chi*, different for example from becoming a spiritual master of *Kung Fu*, which we will see later.

With Christ as your highest master, as your redeemer, you will not fall, in either this life or in the Spirit realm. It is only through emptying yourself of yourself that you ascend and are made in the image of Christ. And in order to realize the higher level of this path, which is direct relationship, you must first experience an awakening, "you must be born again" (John 3:1-21).

Regardless of the level at which you practice this path it is crucial that you be functioning within a spiritual tradition and remaining faithful to it in order to have protection and stability as you go through the experience.

Chapter 18

Awakening and Becoming

Walking the Path of the Spirit

In order to follow the Path of the Spirit you must first awaken. You must therefore enter into rigorous spiritual disciplines, which must of course also be done with self-love and self-care and with inner patience and self-acceptance. There has to be a balance of internal stretch and support, of pushing yourself and giving yourself self-care. Short of a miraculous work of grace, this is a path that involves real effort and dedication.

To communicate the difficulty of this path, I call it "seal training for spiritual wannabes." I'm not joking. In the Christian Orthodox tradition, this is called the way of illumination and likewise involves rigor. You will have to destroy 'yourself' to become yourself, to become your true self, as an awakened and surrendered soul. You must lose your life to find it (Matthew 10:39).

You must become embodied in Spirit.

Nobody else can do it for you and your psychologist or spiritual teacher can only be a support. Money also can't buy this. "Limit experiences," that is to say, experiences that approach the edge of living in terms of their intensity and seeming impossibility, can begin to produce this result. Truth can happen at the limits. This is perhaps best understood by chaos theory, where it is understood that a system has its highest functionality at system limits that can pass into collapse. Highest functionality can happen at the edge, and can produce new realities.

This is the reason why I use the metaphor of "seal training." Special forces training intensives are an example of something that can awaken you. This can also happen as a result of a traumatic accident, a relationship that pushes beyond your coping limits, or a near-death experience. All these can produce awakenings.

That said, I once had an out of body experience during acupuncture, which could not have been a more comfortable experience, so I am not suggesting that it needs to be traumatic. I do not suggest that you simulate these experiences because this can result in spiritually toxic outcomes or even spiritual abuse. Still, there is the necessity of breaking down egoic structures. There has to be a reset that lasts, which is not easy to accomplish; even decades in therapy alone cannot do this.

Waking up is only a prelude to ascent, and to walking the Path of the Son.

Disciplines: Enduring the Path of the Spirit

It is necessary to eliminate the false self for your soul to be released from bondage and for the true self to come into being. To do this, the Buddhists practice negating disciplines such as chanting the Heart Sutra, "no eyes, no ears, no nose, no mouth, no body, no mind." They operate in a *reality-densifying container of silence for sometimes weeks on end, meditating with a focus on breathing for up to seven hours a day.* In this way they negate egoic structures within the supportive container of a practicing community, producing awakening.

This works. It worked for me after doing it for months. There are now some few groups of Christians who practice Zen, who are spread across Europe and the United States, and I hope this will eventually become a network also in Asia which can be the basis for dedicated community practice, including Orthodox reading and prayer methods. As you have seen, one of the founding assertions of this book is that the collective practice of spiritual disciplines is essential now more than ever, and is a solid foundation for revival in America.

The Zen meditation method is highly disciplined, and thus effective. The sitting postures require physical as well as psychological discipline, and so help the mind to focus and align as well. When I first came to Zen —having already lived on a Tibetan monastery in Yorkshire— I was still unprepared for the Zen intensives, called "sesshin" that I experienced at *la Gendronniere* Zen monastery in France. The pain of sitting the lotus position for hours was excruciating. My hip sockets felt like they were going to fall out, the upright posture made my whole body shake, and the sweat from the pain would drip off my chin while my feet went to sleep. It was terrible, but I did it.

Therefore, I caution that you build up to this, starting by sitting daily for 30 minutes in the positions illustrated in the graphics at the end of the book. If the posture recommended by Zen is too difficult for you, sit down in a comfortable chair, but with a firm back —keep your back upright— and focus only on your breathing, letting thoughts pass as if on a screen, keeping your eyes slightly open and your gaze at a downward angle, ideally facing toward a blank surface. Throw your shoulders back and keep your back straight and your spine aligned; don't slouch. If you choose to do a personal retreat, do it alternating between 25 minutes of meditation and 10 minutes of fast walking. Maintain centered focus. Don't fall asleep, and use a timer. Quit if you have to, but keep precisely to this structure. Don't let meditation sessions get undisciplined on the edges. Do this for 12-24 hours if you can without falling asleep, getting up otherwise only to go to the bathroom and hydrate.

Follow this by shorter periods of meditation during the week period, at least 5 hours a day during a seven-day limited fast in which you function in silence, with relative sensory deprivation. This can also be done effectively out in nature, but if you are indoors it is helpful to have an altar for focus and orientation. Light a candle and meditate on scripture pre-selected in advance. Reading spiritual poetry that has layered depth can also be useful. Your mind is very open to experiencing spiritual insight this state. A couple of times a day, but not more, you can open the scriptures to a random spot and see what presents to your consciousness, if a word or phrase comes to you with special meaning. This can give you additional material for reflection and enrich your times of prayer.

During your retreat, you should have a psychologist that is available and sympathetic to your desires and intents. I recommend Jungian therapists for this because of the kind of spiritual material that can emerge during this process. If you practice Yoga this can also be grounding, along with taking walks in nature. Don't stop if the results from the first retreat are mixed. Do it again. There are of course shorter versions of this and similar daily practice that you can start with until you can do an extended period of retreat. Make sure you have spiritual and emotional support.

Something simple you can also do in daily life that opens you out onto the synchronicity of reality is a simple concentration discipline. While it is simple, it is also powerful. It is one that they train for within intelligence agencies. Try it: go into a "container environment" like a cafe, where there are people coming and going, having conversations, regular and occasional visitors, staff. First, focus on your breathing and reach a very calm, centered state. Always arrive to a situation with your full self, but empty of self-intention. It is only in this way that you can actually see what is happening. You cannot come with an agenda if you want to see the situation most clearly. Start with the primary thing being the encounter itself. Then try to take in the full sense of the environment; what is the general overview of what is happening?

Observe specific scenarios occurring around you and try to hold what is happening in mind as you take in more of the environment. What color is the wall, what drink did the man order, why is that woman tilting her head in that way, what does she want from that conversation? Once you have captured the overall sense and ongoing specifics, then try to raise questions, such as: what is missing? What is different? Is someone or something out of place? You might even encounter the true nature of someone, their "true face," as it is called in Buddhism. Perhaps in a flash, out of the corner of your eye, you will see your answers. My Zen teacher in France, Roland Rech, gives the useful example of riding a bicycle and having the forward concentration required to drive, but also the diffuse observation to see peripheral things happening. The point here is to be focused on the particular and the immediate but also to experience the surrounding whole.

This whole is a perfectly orchestrated puzzle that flows together with everyone's diverse intentions, mingling and creating the holographic reality in which you are absorbed. This experience is often naturally occurring in the awakened mind, which is why I suggest it as an exercise. There is not one quark or particle that does not impact the whole; the "butterfly effect" is true. You are experiencing the content of the Divine Mind in which you can be a prime mover. You can be, that is, a fully unlocked soul embodied in Spirit.

This happens all the way down to dealing with numbers. Every number has a meaning and this also is something you can be aware of. It is intrinsic to the Jewish mystical practices. Numbers reveal the simple elegance of the universe, and can be integrated into practice. Above the level of numbers is symbology, which is the discovery of meaning of even the objects around you. In semiotics this is treated as the sign, signifier and the signified, but is this beyond the scope of what we are covering here. Taken together, everything from the billboard to the coffee cup have a synchronistic place, and with a certain amount of discipline you can begin to experience what is around you like an abstract map of intuitive data, the reading of which can result in the ability in some rare cases to intuit immediate and future events, to connect to other spiritual realities.

Here I would caution not to grasp onto anything, that is, not to latch on to a particular piece of data too much, not to let your *desire to decipher* destroy your peripheral view, but to just practice catch and release, non-attachment. If it matters, it will come up for you later and be useful, so do not allow this to distort your thinking or for you to become fixated on specific material or things. If you do have these experiences, resist the need to immediately share these with people who are not close and supportive. If you do not have these experiences it in no way suggests you are not a spiritual person.

The second practical exercise I would recommend, which is related, is listening for inauthenticity or double meanings in communications. It's a kind of "what are they really saying" exercise at the depth level. You may have used this or become aware of this when you were talking with someone, where the conversation is about something completely different, but the words communicated romantic intentions, or, on the other hand, perhaps the tone or content masked an underlying argument or complaint.

The French famously call this kind of double meaning a "double entendre," and yet the British are perhaps the best masters with their own witticisms. What is happening with wit is that you are turning meanings, finding a true meaning or absurdity at the deeper level of communication. It's often hilarious. Every great comedian must do this. While it doesn't seem to be the objective here, keep in mind that entering into the deeper levels of meaning, and the revealing of false egoic structures, is not always a "heavy," "sad," "deep" experience. It will often make you laugh. One of the awesome things about awaking is *criterionless* laughter.

Some linguists have argued that underneath all languages runs a current of reasoning that is intrinsic to the human mind. The awakened mind automatically functions at this deeper level and so sees the untruth in communication, which is what is hidden in the soul that subconsciously expresses itself in conversation. Intelligent people can do this too and a good psychologist should be able to do this, but the person who is not completely purified also brings their own distortions to the process. In therapy, this can result in transference and countertransference, along with a range of other therapeutic impediments.

Language itself has the power to determine us by giving us fixed constructs with which to think, and thereby altering our mental states. In some way I am a different person when speaking French than when speaking English. One of the things I suggest to break down these constructs is to learn another language, or study etymology. Language presents us with an excellent example of the challenges in communicating truth, and is thus one of the constructs that must be broken down, and rationally deconstructed. The awakened mind does this without thinking. It does it, that is, through "thinking non-thinking," as it is called in Zen. *What is the sound of one hand clapping?*

A more difficult exercise you can do with another person is to choose a topic of conversation and have a conversation about something different while within the original topic, doing this to the point that the secondary stream of communication could be denied as having ever happened. This method relates to neurolinguistic programming, a psychological method for introducing thoughts into other people's mind and shifting their concentration without their conscious awareness. Because of this, it is important to have disciplines for personal protection. Still, this happens impersonally all the time with something as mundane as marketing. This sort of thing is happening at the preconscious level and we don't even realize it. A lot of repressed material and internal meaning lives just below the surface.

Helping people break through these layers is part of the task of the spiritual psychologist. Just as the disciplined exercise of following a tradition in complete mindfulness can in the negative become an obsessive-compulsive disorder, similarly functioning within the disciplines of awakening can in the negative lead to psychosis, and to paranoia. Remember, the mystic and the schizophrenic swim in the same water. Don't drown, get support. Pray for inner purity.

One final fun thing I would suggest that you do is to keep a diary that has a simple record of daily happenings, where you were, what you were doing, what kinds of issues you were working through, and reference back to them each year. In both the traditions of the East and also in the Jewish mystical tradition there is belief in and use of astrology. The ancients were keenly aware of this and this is how the Persian magi, or magicians, were able to find Christ according to the New Testament. In the Ancient Greek tradition, there is the story of Abaris the skywalker, who, following the *hyperborea,* moved in circles around the land, teaching, his paths repeating their concentric circles. This was part of his way of teaching ultimate truth. This is the truth of planetary cycles, and also of our daily lives. An awakened person will be aware of this.

Essentially, our daily life functions upon the same principle as the transmigration of the soul over lifetimes, but within the container of a single lifetime; thus, there is a trace of this repetition even in the simplest patterns of our lives. You finally must harmonize with the whole while also overcoming within it, learning from your past mistakes and refinements.

To conclude, the discipline I most recommend for awakening in all senses, is Zen meditation (coupled with prayer).

Ascent: Nearing the Summit of the Path of the Spirit

As with the Path of the Father, there are two levels of this practice. The first is awakening, which we have discussed, and the second is ascent. This is the process you must go through to reach additional spiritual levels. I will do my best to make this as simple as possible. First of all, you've got to be entirely honest, internally and externally. Stop lying. Period. You won't get off the launching pad if you can't do this at a depth level. You must enter into purifying authenticity. This is where all the untrue things you tell yourself to make things okay, stops.

This will inevitably hurt. But just be the flower you are. What do I mean by that?

Well, if you're a simple rose, completely accept that at a deep level. If, on the other hand, you are a hydrangea that only blooms under special conditions, become that with all that it entails. Only when you accept the core DNA of your soul, which is your true self now partially revealed through your awakening, can your DNA begin to be transformed. For this to happen you have to get rid of the false self. You must become real.

Part of this also is recognizing and being compassionate toward, being in a dance with, that which you do not wish to be, your shadow. You will have to transform the base elements into gold and this can be done by anyone, but the process will be as unique as you are. It will be difficult but you can finally expect to become something amazing, just as you are with none of the extras you thought you needed.

A simple prayer that I recommend here is King David's prayer, *"create in me a clean heart, O God; and renew a right spirit within me, cast me not away from thy presence; and take not thy Holy Spirit from me."* Keep praying this. Your spiritual ascent depends upon it. It is both relational and about surrender. This is not some abstract exercise, so don't ever pray it that way. Don't drive the Spirit away with prayers that are not heartfelt. Pray that you can pray if you must, or even be angry if that is where you are, but do it, or be it, with your whole being.

One thing you might consider doing, which has been central to my own practice, is to think of yourself as having a spiritual hand on either side. One hand is judgment, the other hand is mercy. Internalize this. As I was going through this process I would feel a burning in the palm of my left hand and in this way knew that my Spirit was experiencing judgment, either internally or externally, that something discriminating was happening. When I felt a burning in my right palm I knew that I was expressing internally, often not to my conscious knowledge, compassion or mercy. Sometimes I feel a burning in both my hands and feet.

The Godself —the Soul of G-d, as we saw in Paths of the Trinity— is agency with two essential sides, that of justice and wisdom, or Judgment, and of truth and love, or Mercy. It is through balancing these two core energies internally, through experiencing them in oscillation along the ascent of the DNA of our soul, that we climb the ladder of divine ascent with both legs. To use a Star Wars metaphor, "there are two sides to the Force." We need spiritual Jedi in this age.

As we suggested above, wisdom without love is dangerous, but love that is not expressed with wisdom can become useless and can result in the oppression of the righteous in this world as it is now. This is a trap that many very spiritual people fall into, and which ignores the Path of the Father. The Path of the Spirit requires harmony and balance, lived internally on all levels. It is as simple as that. Wisdom without love, is dangerous. To avoid that danger, and to avoid a useless practice, what I have offered here are simple solutions and methods which have worked for me.

If it works, it works. Overthinking can be a spiritual trap. As we have seen throughout, the Spirit is in all things and the Divine energies present everywhere. Understanding and working with these energies is an essential part of being on the Path of the Spirit and of embodying in Spirit.

A discipline I recommend for energy work is Taoism, beginning with Tai Chi. On the advice of the teacher Deng Ming-Dao, I had planned to go to China to study with Master Bing, but this did not work out due to my collapse. However, Christianity and Taoism have intermingled historically in China for over 1000 years. In 1907 in China, explorers discovered ancient scrolls dating from the 5th to 11th centuries —the *Jesus Sutras*— recounting a history of Jesus' life and teachings in Taoist concepts unknown in the West. I am not suggesting these texts are authoritative, but it is my view that Paths of the Trinity is a Taoism. However, without the Path of the Son there is no redemption and without 'death to self' there is no final *theosis*. Without standing in the redemptive mercy of God, within the harmony of the Trinity, even a great master will eventually fall in this life or the next.

The Christian Kabbalist tradition has also been part of inner Christianity since the medieval ages and, along with Christian Hermeticism, is the *ethos* of this book. This tradition is the contemporary connection with the 1st century Christian Merkabah tradition that runs in parallel with my own revelation, and is the historical Christian connection to what I have written. As we have seen already, Jewish mysticism is the ancient core of Christian mystical practice.

Therefore, working with the paths of the Sefirot, memorizing and internalizing them, using these methods to produce inner harmony and ascent, is unsurprisingly a related spiritual practice. A very accessible and insightful introductory book about this that I recommend is "God is a Verb: Kabbalah and the Practice of Mystical Judaism" by Rabbi David Cooper. That said, in historical Christian Kabbalism, Christ is represented at the crown of the Sephirot, and thus in this practice to embody this form is finally to embody Christ. This does not take into full consideration, in my view, the necessity of self-emptying and self-sacrifice, or redemption, which is the essential movement on the Path of the Son, as we shall see towards conclusion.

In the Christian Kabbalist tradition there is also an understanding of levels or worlds, related to layers of soul, but what is important to understand is that what is happening here, now, correlates with, and has an active impact between worlds. Consider, for example, the laws of correspondence, summed up in the Hermetic phrase "as above so below." Up until now I have loosely talked about the "Spirit realm" and have discussed, briefly, how heavens and hells interact, and that they interpenetrate with our own reality. In Catholicism there is the belief in "Purgatory," a realm where souls are purified of their misdeeds, and it is in this realm that Saints and others are working to help us during our lives on this earth. This is part of the Spirit realm.

What I recommend in terms of the Christian Hermetic tradition is this: pay attention to when something you think or do results in a shift in the Spirit realm, and to when the opposite is true as well. Your life directly impacts souls there. Souls there— Saint and ancestors—are working with you. It is possible to observe what is happening here and to infer what is happening there, but what is most important to understand is that there is an intermingling between worlds, "as above, so below." Getting this is the source of miracles.

However, it is not necessary to use these sophisticated practices to ascend. Kabbalism is indeed an especially powerful, complex tradition in its own right, one which would require a separate and much longer manuscript than what fits the purposes of the present essay. The simple tools I have offered so far are enough if applied with heart and dedication. This will become more clear as we look at the practical applications of living The Path of the Son.

Following the Path of the Spirit results in what the Christian Orthodox tradition calls *theoria*, or illumination, and is what is called *sanctification* in the Protestant Holiness Tradition. The results of following this path are authenticity and internal harmony and will produce spiritual ascent, which can finally result in theosis, spiritual completion through fully realizing the Path of the Son.

Chapter 19

Self-Emptying and Self-Sacrifice: Walking the Path of the Son

Whereas above we learned about the Path of the Father, and the Path of the Spirit, here, our explication of the Paths of the Trinity begins to take final shape as we develop what we have established regarding the Path of the Son. The Path of the Son, lived internally, can be summed up in the admonishment "fix your eyes upon Jesus." Christ said that we must be like children to learn of him who is "meek and lowly of heart" (Matthew 11:29). This is the way of the heart. It is love and mercy, and kindness lived internally, self-sacrifice and self-emptying. It is picking up your cross and following Christ. It is simple to understand, but difficult to actualize.

The "broken and contrite spirit God will not despise" (Psalm 51:17). And it is in this Spirit that you enter into Divine Grace. On the path of the heart, you will ascend most quickly by praying for others and by giving of yourself. By living without condemnation. By extending grace and mercy. If you do the opposite, namely, if you cling to the egoic self or judgment without entire self-emptying, short of fully embodying the fruits of the Spirit, "love, joy, peace, patience, kindness, goodness, faithfulness, gentleness, and self-control," you will fall like I did. But falling is not all bad, especially if finally it is to be remade "in his image and likeness" (Genesis 1:27) and allows you to put on the mind of Christ. Unfaltering trust in Divine Providence is necessary to walk the path of faith, so do not be discouraged or dismayed if you happen to fall (Psalm 43:5, Deuteronomy 31:8).

As I have shared, one way to fall is to be a prophet who dwells too much in judgment, which is one part of my own story. In the age of predator capitalism —in the age of the evangelical prosperity gospel— many Christians could not be further from the message of Christ, could not be more distanced from the practices of the early church that were a natural result of embodying the Fruits of the Spirit. This was very difficult for me to reconcile as I began my return to Christianity. It was therefore necessary as part of my spiritual practice after awakening to control intense feelings of prejudice toward Christianity in America, and I sometimes lived with spiritually toxic levels of judgment toward Evangelical Christianity.

Merle Haggard has a great song, "you're walking on the fightin' side of me," which is about how he reacted when people criticized America. According to him, if you don't like it you should leave it, which is exactly what I had done. I had been very disappointed by how our country treats the weak, the disabled, the veterans, and the homeless whose well-being is part of our mission as Christians (Matthew 25:40). However, God sent me back to the United States from the French Riviera, from the life I had chosen.

God sent me back from a place that provided work and dignity for veterans and the disabled, back from a country that placed the mentally-ill in jobs rather than eventually in prisons. God sent me back whether I wanted to go or not. I got so sick I had no choice. I got spewed up on the beach, just like Jonah before me, and also with a message.

This message is that Christian America must repent of how it treats "the least of these" and it must stop projecting the negative onto the other, and instead, enter into real spiritual disciplines. Christianity must enter into a new era of living the inner life, rather than the outer garments of our tradition. This must happen within the life of the individual, but also within the life of the church. It is time to build Christian communities dedicated to walking the Path of the Son.

As I shared earlier, Christ and the early church were pacifists who lived in community, giving to "each according as anyone had need" (Acts 4:35). This is the logical result of living out the Fruits of the Spirit, of actually following Christ's message and living out the Path of the Son. Living in this way begins the Kingdom of God realized here on earth, in community.

But is it possible to live out this life of sharing, this life of community, against the backdrop of the highly individualized political and economic reality of today? Yes; it is being done by many who are living out this message. How do I know this? This year, in 2017, I spent time with the Bruderhof, a group of believers who are communitarians, who live in community as did the early church. They have communities on multiple continents, including Latin America and Australia. I worked at their factory in upstate New York and also at their location in the United Kingdom, in East Sussex.

I stood in the assembly lines and put parts together. I shared in family meals and drank homemade beer. I lived this life myself. I saw with my own eyes that this can work. What I learned from this is that not only is community a workable model, but in community, one can enjoy both real and simple abundance. Of course, every human arrangement is determined by the limits of social structures and tradition, and in community there can also be loneliness. Social structures can become alienating and oppressive, and without spiritual disciplines such as dedicated prayer and meditation a community can become spiritually lifeless. However, these obstacles can be overcome. Living according to models such as these is to begin to realize Christ's Kingdom now, and this is precisely what it is to follow the Path of the Son as a Christian community.

Towards concluding this essay, I wish to share my vision for Christianity in North America. My vision is that there will be a fundamental shift in consciousness, a collective awakening as a result of following spiritual disciplines and that this awakening will motivate Christians to follow Christ within community. I envision that Christians will support local communities with diverse forms of shared ownership, witness them as "spiritual containers" that can be alive and welcoming. Of course, these communities must also be structured to protect those whose sacrifices have made these fragile new patterns of human consciousness possible.

Now is the time for Christians to collectively follow the path of Christ and of the early church. This is the age when it is possible; we have more collective prosperity and wealth than at any other recorded time in human history. We can do this, because we can share this. Now is the time to enter into spiritual disciplines and Christian community. This does not mean that everyone must live in community or that reasonable wealth is intrinsically wrong; but remember that the final movement is self-sacrifice and self-emptying. It is not the wealth that we possess —either spiritual or otherwise— but how we choose to use it, how we bear the weight of this responsibility (Matthew 19:24). Can we do this entirely to the Glory of God?

Whereas on the general Path of the Spirit there is personal empowerment and internal harmony, on the specific Path of the Son you must live your entire life as a profound giving, you must experience brokenness, and you must finally realize that your beautiful DNA is paradoxically still short of the mark of absolute perfection, still short of completion in perfect love and mercy. It is only through self-sacrifice and self-emptying, a total giving of all you have unconditionally in complete love that you will become complete. Sainthood is possible for everyone in this lifetime, and as Christians, it is our calling (1Corinthians 1:2). You must become in the image of Christ. Redemption is possible in this lifetime.

The German philosopher Nietzsche saw self-emptying as being the final effects of becoming the "ubermensch," or overman. He imagined that this person would have such an excess of being that this would spill out beyond good and evil, as a supreme gifting. And yet, he did not see Christ as being just that. What he saw instead was the Christianity of his day. He only saw Christians, not people becoming Christ. How many more great Spirits are similarly alienated from Christianity today? We bear collective responsibility for this. Today's Christianity turns people away from Christ. It happened to me. It happens to millions more.

Whereas on the Path of the Spirit you risk becoming an empowered spiritual being that will be defeated, on the Path of the Son you are safe. However, this only happens through self-sacrifice and standing in Christ's mercy. Here the highest Self is born. Find your ascent in the harmony of the Trinity, as surrendered imperfection, humbled before God. The highest truth is God's glory in love and it is through this gift of being, which happens beyond time in an eternal now, that we have our individual consciousness.

Perfection is possible but wisdom is only made perfect in love. Even in the heavens we ascend to higher truths and become into greater glory with God in Spirit. Like others before have observed, including the great Protestant mystic Immanuel Swedenborg, I am confident this journey is only one of many and continues eternally. So have faith that "all things work together for the good of them that love God" and remember that "the joy of the Lord is your strength" (Romans 8:28, Nehemiah 8:10).

Christ challenged us, "be ye holy as I am holy." Sonship in Christ is thus to become a perfect son of God embodied in love. To become divinized in love is to become the perfect face of God, that of Mercy, becoming Christ. This is the highest calling and to which we are each called. This is the mind of Christ. This is the theosis.

Come to Christ just as you are. Broken with nothing more.

Chapter 20

Conclusion

In this little book I have communicated to you, dear unknown friend, many essential things. I have given you this little book which is the result of much suffering. I am handing the baton to you. You have seen the mission, you have seen the calling, you have seen the discipline. Now it is up to you to put all this into practice. I'm not a pastor, I'm not a priest, and I'm barely a scribe. I'm just a humble man fulfilling his calling, and transferring to you yours. Now it is up to you to realize this within yourself and out in the world. It is up to you, dear unknown friend. I am handing you the baton.

Tear out the following pages, and get to work.

Stick with It

Live life

as a confessional

But don't just spit

it all out

And don't beat yourself up

It's not about you

A gesture here

an implicit apology there

an opened door

a watered flower

Let the universe know

you're with it

Stick with it

You'll be amazed

You will

wake up

ESTABLISHING A **SOLID BASE**, WHAT WE CALL A *THREE POINT SUSPENSION*, JACK IS GETTING INTO WHAT WE CALL THE *BURMESE POSTURE*. THIS IS AN EASY POSTURE BUT CAN BE QUITE ADEQUATE.

HE BEGINS TO SEAT HIMSELF BY EXTENDING HIS RIGHT LEG CLOCKWISE TO HIS BODY,

HE BRINGS HIS LEFT LEG IN, WITH THE TOP OF HIS FOOT IN CONTACT WITH THE MAT.

THEN TUCKS HIS HEEL UNDER HIS CROTCH.

NOW HIS KNEES ARE STABLE AND CAN SUPPORT HIS WEIGHT EVENLY.

ONCE YOUR KNEES ARE STABLE AND ON THE MAT, YOU SHIFT SOME OF YOUR WEIGHT ONTO THEM AND GET THE THIRD POINT, YOUR BUTT, ALIGNED.

NEXT, WE *ERECT THE SPINE*, LET OUR GUT *RELAX....*

WE MAY FIND OUR BACK TENDS TO CURVE FORWARD, WE *SLOUCH*.

ADDING MORE CUSHION UNDER THE BUTT ADDS SUPPORT OUR THREE POINTS ARE SET...

NOW WE GET OUR **BACK** INTO FORM.

WITH PRACTICE, THE MUSCLES WHICH HOLD US IN AN *ERECT* AND *REGAL POSTURE* WILL *STRENGTHEN*.

117

AND OPEN UP OUR *CHEST AREA* BY MOVING OUR SHOULDERS BACK.

A FRIEND WHO TAUGHT ME YOGA USED TO SAY:

"IMAGINE YOU HAVE *ANGEL WINGS*, AND SPREAD THEM OUT."

A NICE OVAL IS FORMED WITH THE PALMS AND THUMBS...

THE PRESSURE OF THE THUMBS TOGETHER IS *VERY LIGHT....*

YOU SHOULD BE ABLE TO SLIDE A PIECE OF PAPER BETWEEN THEM,

LIKE YOU WERE *GAPPING THE POINTS* ON A CAR...

THAT'S HOW YOU GET YOUR BODY IN *CORRECT POSTURE.*

NOW OUR *ZAZEN PRACTICE* CAN. BEGIN...

TO BE CONTINUED...

If this book has inspired you to begin meditation disciplines, please consider joining the Zen Christian Network, an online community site with a geographic feature that allows people to form physical groups in their area and to begin practice together: **http://zenchristiannetwork.org/**

If you have been helped by this book, please also consider giving a charitable donation to our nonprofit. We are dedicated to the promotion, dissemination, and translation of this book, as well as to the eventual development of training centers. *We give many books away for free.*

You can contact us by email: **pathoftrinity@gmail.com**

We need your help to continue to make a difference.